Monks and Love
in Twelfth-Century
France

Monks and Love in Twelfth-Century France

——

Psycho-Historical Essays

——

JEAN LECLERCQ

OXFORD
AT THE CLARENDON PRESS
1979

Oxford University Press, Walton Street, Oxford OX2 6DP

OXFORD LONDON GLASGOW
NEW YORK TORONTO MELBOURNE WELLINGTON
KUALA LUMPUR SINGAPORE JAKARTA HONG KONG TOKYO
DELHI BOMBAY CALCUTTA MADRAS KARACHI
NAIROBI DAR ES SALAAM CAPE TOWN

Published in the United States by
Oxford University Press, New York

© *Oxford University Press* 1979

British Library Cataloguing in Publication Data

Leclercq, Jean
  Monks and Love in twelfth-century France
  1. Love (Theology)—History of doctrines
  2. Love in literature   3. French literature—
  To 1500—History and criticism   4. Christianity
  and literature
  I. Title
  231'.6'0944   BV4639   78-40484
  ISBN 0-19-822546-6

Printed in Great Britain
at the University Press, Oxford
by Eric Buckley
Printer to the University

PREFACE

THIS short series of Essays has its origin in a set of papers read at Oxford University in February 1977. They were first planned to be part of a broader project: a comparative study of love literatures—monastic and secular—in twelfth-century France. But Professor Michael Wallace-Hadrill, who had invited me to Oxford, further extended his courtesy in suggesting that the papers be published where they had been delivered. I am grateful to him for both the invitation and his suggestion, and take the opportunity here of thanking him.

These essays are but the first beginnings of the total project, the complete book, already conceived in my mind, but which may remain unfinished. Any homogeneity in the following pages arises from a singleness of approach which is psycho-historical, as the Introduction briefly points out, and from the central figure, Bernard of Clairvaux.

The Epilogue, read at Columbia University, New York, in the course of a Dante programme, has been added because it attempts to suggest why and how the feminine presence is important not only in the writings of Dante, but also in those of St. Bernard and many other monastic love poets.

I also wish to thank those who helped me to prepare the manuscript: Sr. Mary Stephen, O.S.B., of St. Mary's Abbey, Fernham, Great Britain; Sr. Gregory, O.S.B., of Penneni Hills, Australia; Sr. Marie Bernard Said, O.S.B., of Oriocourt, France; and Fr. Jacques Winandy, O.S.B., who corrected the proofs.

May 1978

CONTENTS

I

Introduction. Modern Psychology and the Medieval Psyche

STRICTLY speaking, this title is not correct. We cannot reduce modern psychology to a single unity, for it is legion: there are numerous and varied 'psychologies'. Among these there are two major methodological groups.[1] It is frequently supposed that modern methods in psychology are restricted to the observation of human behaviour. The interpretation of such observed behaviour is left to psycho-analysis. But, in fact, practically every form of contemporary psychology implies some element of hermeneutics and, so to speak, of exegesis.

Furthermore, these different psychologies—physiological psychology, behaviourism, neo-behaviourism, Gestalt psychology, introspection, developmental or genetic psychology, phenomenology, structuralism, as well as Jungian, Freudian, neo-Jungian, and neo-Freudian methods—must necessarily work in collaboration with other human sciences such as history, sociology, linguistics, and comparative studies in religion. All this offers the inquiring mind a very complex network. But careful reflection reveals that many of those approaches seem to have in common three factors. The first of them is the importance attributed to the unconscious underlying the surface level of conscious expression. The second fact flows quite naturally from the first: the attention given to language as an expression of the psyche and consequently the necessity of what is called 'psycho-linguistics'. The third common factor would seem to be the study of man's communication and relationship with his environment.

There is, however, a fundamental obstacle to the application of any of the modern psychological methods to the medieval psyche: psychology as it is conceived of today is anthropocentric: it leads us more to man than to God. Now faith in God was a fundamental component of the medieval psyche. Certainly it is true that some of the more broadminded among present-day theorists stress the importance of the fact that man is future-oriented and value-striving. But none will admit initially that there may be in man some more-than-human values.

What is more, not only did the medieval people have a God-oriented psyche, but they also had their own psychologies, that is to say, they had their own sciences of observation, explanation, and interpretation of human behaviours. These psychologies varied from one period or milieu to another. Some were very elaborate and even sophisticated. These were favoured by philosophers and theorists and tended, quite understandably, to be rather abstract. But there were others, especially among monastic spiritual writers, which proposed an insightful and systematic reflection on man as a human person, filled with ambition and ever striving to surpass himself. Such writers showed how this related to concrete behaviour in the day-to-day living out of man's existence.

Our purpose in these present pages is not to make a comparative study of medieval and modern psychologies, but rather to see how the latter can give us a deeper understanding of the medieval psyche and the explanations given by medieval theorists. Before going into the matter, it is essential to point out two facts which existed not only in the medieval psyche itself, but also in the men who attempted some interpretation of it. Though these facts are not specific to the middle ages alone, they are not accepted by all modern systems of psychology. These two suppositions are first that man is a spiritual being, not bound up by his instincts and environment, and secondly that he is naturally religious, that is to say that God exists and that man can enter into relation with him.

Thus, *a priori*, we must exclude the application to the medieval psyche of certain modern psychological interpretations which exclude the spiritual nature of man and the existence of God. Even after having made this distinction in modern psychologies, rejecting some and retaining others, we must be wary of the use we make of those methods which are applicable to medieval man, for certain pitfalls await the incautious. One of these dangers is that of transferring indiscriminately the interpretations of our own age and culture to another quite different one. For example, the mechanism of 'double meanings'—so important in some modern psychologies—is not at all the same as the search for 'hidden meanings' which was part of medieval exegesis of sacred and profane texts. Similarly, any attempt to recognize a Jungian archetype such as 'the feminine' in medieval people, writings, or institutions could be only arbitrary and artificial: we would possibly project the archetype on to the medieval context rather than draw it out from it.

Nevertheless, much is to be gained from all modern approaches. Behaviourism, for instance, is most useful for describing certain psychic phenomena, and these can fitly be interpreted by other methods provided that the medievalist remains sufficiently independent of them to give as much respectful and faithful attention to the text upon which he is working as a psychologist or psychiatrist to his client. Much of what Canon Vergote of the University of Louvain, an authority on religious psychology today, has written in 'Psycho-analysis and Biblical Interpretation' applies to the study of medieval texts: discernment of the unconscious, new attention given to certain modes of expression and certain symbols, new resources for historical criticism in the field of the authenticity of texts, of the literary genres, of the difference between spontaneous language and thought and the written and artistic expression of it, and other points.[2] The use of certain schemes and vocabularies may serve as working hypotheses to ask the texts questions one would never have thought of merely with the aid of methods used in purely historical criticism. For example, the use of Marxist or of neo-Marxist methods of fact analysis, independently of the ideo-logies with which they are associated, has already proved fruitful in the field of biblical exegesis. In the same way, a new reading of medieval documents in the light of modern psychologies is worth trying and has already brought some results.

After these preliminaries, I can now start to expound my method of approach resulting from seminar work with psycho-logists of different orientations. Let us admit at the outset that every 'psychology' is a system of beliefs and, therefore, requires, so to speak, a faith. This applies both to the methods used, and, with regard to the middle ages, to the object of study, namely a psyche of which faith is an element. Now, what is there in the psyche that can become matter for historical study?

The first fact to be borne in mind when examining the medieval psyche is that we are dealing with human beings similar to our-selves. Medieval spiritual literature does not reveal the existence of men from outer space. The writings which have come down to us from the middle ages were produced by beings of our own planet, but in circumstances which differed from those of this last quarter of our twentieth century. Thus, the question to be asked is whether the conjunctures of medieval times affected the medieval psyche. If so, to what extent? In order to give a satis-factory answer we may posit human needs as being on three levels: the physiological, the psycho-sociological, and the spiri-tual. Such needs are universally invariable independently of any fluctuating circumstance. However, according to variations in the cultural context, one or other of these needs may well be submitted to social pressures in the control or expression of the emotions to which it gives rise. Thus, for example, in a particular race or other ethnical group, aggression might well be a condition of survival, and therefore in the scale of values taught to children it will rate high. In other groups, however, where the fight for survival is less keen, by reason of more clement circumstances, it will be some more pacific value which will receive the higher rating. Man's needs are universally the same. It is the orchestration of these needs which changes. Hence the necessity of elaborating a theory which considers man as a composite being fashioned by the interaction of his natural endowments and his environment. This approach, though relatively new, has already been used by psychologists in the study of what is called 'moral development' or 'ego development'. It is very difficult to establish scientifically the truth of any theory in psychology. Generally speaking, however, it would seem evident that if we set out from a narrow philosophical premiss of the coefficient between stimulus and response, we shall come to more restricted conclusions than those based on a broader premiss. Though such conclusions may have been to a certain extent theoretically predictable, they will have a higher degree of experimental veracity due to the wider views on which they were initially based. Thus we may, and I think we must, admit that as human beings we have certain *needs* which in interaction with our environment form our personality. The determinant factors in man's environmental experiences are those he has in his own family and culture. This fact explains why so many theorists find it difficult to give much credit to Freud's rigid interpretation of sexual symbols: these have different meanings in different cultures. Freud himself recognized sexuality as being polymorphous: it is not an isolated element in human nature, but influences, variously, every sphere of man's activity. At all periods of history we commonly and constantly notice that, on the whole, women have different thought processes than men, and this simply because they have two opposing and complementary sexualities. Consequently, by way of example, a sermon by Bernard of Clairvaux or Gilbert of Hoyland on the verse of the Song of Songs describing the breasts of the bride will inevitably call forth different reactions if read in a choir of monks than it would if read in a choir of nuns. The cognitive function of St. Theresa of Avila differed from that of St. John of the Cross because she was a woman and he a man. But both are saints and doctors of the Church and they shared an identical spiritual experience.

The question revolves on how seriously we take the unity of

man into consideration. Is man nothing but a *tabula rasa* on which events and men leave their mark, or is he a flower which gradually blossoms under internal genetic pressure? I prefer to think, as I have already mentioned above, that he is structured psychologically by the interaction of his environment and his endowments. If we adopt this last hypothesis we admit that a man's endowments and his environment are structurally distinct. The more or less harmonious interplay of these distinctive structures results in a totally new structure, the individual personality.

In conclusion we may affirm, in the first place, that any interpretation of the psyche, be it modern, medieval, or of any other age, will be a function of our basic psychological premiss. If the human being is merely a socially determined animal then we have nothing to learn by the study of the medieval psyche. On the other hand, if we approach man as a being with specific needs interrelating with environment, then history has much to teach us.

A second conclusion concerns the nature of history, which, in the light of the foregoing theory, is seen to be the study not only of the inter-relationship between man's endowments and environment but also of the way in which human needs are orchestrated. Music is always music at any age, whatever audible form it may have. We can therefore still tune in to the harmonies of medieval people and medieval writers. Occasionally the song or air may jar on our nerves or shock our sense of propriety—for example, when Saint Catherine of Siena organizes a crusade in an attempt to save Europe—because today our ears prefer a more gentle, pacific song. Even so, in our own modern symphonies we still find the harsher strident notes of aggressiveness, because we, like our forebears, must cope with and sublimate our own aggressive forces.

Concerning sexuality too, we may remark that St. Hildegard, St. Bernard, and other medieval saints in no way denied the reality of their bodily nature and their psychological make-up. They assumed them and spoke of them unconsciously and with astonishing frankness. In every time and place, sexuality is socially controlled, and in recent centuries in Western Europe, one method of control has been a certain refusal to recognize its power as a determinant of man's behaviour. However, we must distinguish between a person's interior, willed denial of an emotional pattern, and the exterior social control of its expression. It is precisely in the sphere of social control that the middle ages differ from later centuries.

This brings us to the third and final conclusion: one of the purposes of history is to study the evolution of social controls. Such study is not, of course, restricted to the social control of human expressions of sexuality. It examines everything by which man manifests himself as a person—anger, affection, the rearing of children, etc. History is concerned with the variations occurring from one century to another of those formative experiences by which a people or a specific culture expresses its basic needs in terms of a value system.

Man is not totally determined by society and social control. He can therefore, while still conforming to social ethics, express his basic needs in an individual manner. The resulting melody will inevitably vary from one individual to another—and even vary for the same individual at different periods of his life-span—even for persons living in the same culture and period of history.

It is this theory of personality construction by the interaction of endowments and environment that I would like to apply to the medieval psyche as manifested by the love literature produced in twelfth-century France by monks, particularly St. Bernard of Clairvaux.

[1] A. Vergote, 'Psychanalyse et interprétation biblique', in *Dictionnaire de la Bible. Supplément*, fasc. 41–50A, Paris, 1975, cols. 252–60.

[2] In two previous papers, the content of which is not repeated here, I have discussed the general problems indicated by their titles: 'Modern Psychology and the Interpretation of Medieval Texts', *Speculum*, 48 (1973), pp. 476–90; 'Modern Psychology and the Understanding of Medieval People', *Cistercian Studies*, 11 (1976), pp. 269–89. In the following footnotes, the titles which are not preceded by authors' names are those of publications where I have dealt at greater length with topics which can only be touched on briefly here. Another redaction of the Introduction and Chapter V, or parts of these texts, has appeared in *Indiana Social Studies Quarterly*, 30 (1977), pp. 5–26, and is reproduced here with permission of the editors of this journal.

II

New Recruitment—New Psychology

THE point of this essay is to compare the different realities denoted by the word love—love between one human being and another, love between human beings and God—in two different milieux: secular society and monastic society. We shall be using sociological categories of expression in an attempt to avoid the ambiguities which tend to cling to the distinctions arising from psychological, moral, or religious norms which require the use of terms such as the profane and the sacred, secular and religious, carnal and spiritual, human and divine, and so forth.

There are many and varied texts telling us about love as it was conceived of in the two milieux we are studying here. For instance, much can be learned about secular love by the perusal of romances by troubadours and trouvères, as well as from fabliaux, letters, poems, and even from texts written by canonists and theologians. Any comparative study must take into account the different forms of literature, including the musical play, all possible sources of inspiration, and the linguistic medium of expression. Languages, themes, images, and geographical facts such as the situation of the major centres of production—Troyes, Poitiers, Orléans, Paris, to mention but a few—are all so many factors to be examined in their psychological, spiritual, theological, and sociological context.

The first of these factors claiming our attention is of the sociological order, for in medieval society, both secular and religious, people were classed according to very rigid categories between which there were almost insurmountable barriers. Possibly the only thing which could overstep these boundaries between the classes was love. Did it actually succeed in doing so? This opens up an extensive field of inquiry which can be approached from various angles. We shall confine ourselves in these pages to examining the extent to which monastic recruitment had any lasting influence on love literature.

God's love for man and man's love for God must needs be expressed in human language borrowed from human images and symbols and ultimately from human experience. The task facing us here is to attempt to discern the basic, primary experience—either personal or collective—of the love of twelfth-century monks and nuns, and the terms in which they expressed it. Both the language and the type of love experience they had were dependent not only on the type of human beings, men and women, that they were, but also on the society—in this particular instance, the monastic society—to which they belonged.

I. *Adult recruitment*

In the twelfth century, within the limits of the same monasticism, there were two different social settings, one we may term 'traditional', the other 'new' monasticism. Traditional monasticism was that where monks (and nuns) lived within the bounds of pre-twelfth-century houses and institutions: in those days they were called black monks and much later were given the name of 'Benedictines'. New monasticism was made up of all members of the monastic or canonical orders which sprang up at the end of the eleventh and in the beginning of the twelfth century. These were Carthusians, principally the Cistercians—the white monks —as well as Augustinian Canons, the Premonstratensians, and the regular canons of St. Victor of Paris. What were the psychosociological differences between these two types of monastic milieux? The major difference issued from the way they recruited new members. In this field, as in any other, we must avoid simplification. We may say, however, that, on the whole, members of the old orders usually drew their recruits from among the oblates, that is to say, the children who had been 'offered' by their parents.[1] Many of these children were sons and daughters of noble families, whose parents, for one reason or another, did not want them to get married but to become monks or nuns.[2] Some of them were handicapped, and for these the monastery was a saving refuge. Herman the Counterfeit, the eleventh-century encyclopedist, a specialist in arithmetic and music, is one example—but one of genius—among others who were never known.[3] Often the parents offered land or a sum of money with the child. Such 'oblates' were educated in the monastic schools and almost all of them passed quite naturally from the school, which was similar to a long noviciate, to the community. The educational system was such that, generally speaking, they became not only good monks, but also happy monks.[4] Doubtless, this state of affairs began to change during the twelfth century, but it did so slowly and in a way which did not greatly modify the psycho-sociological framework of the communities. So it was that the majority of monks and nuns had never known any life other than that of the cloister.

On the other hand, the new orders, for various reasons, were very strict about putting an end to this sort of recruitment. The main reason was a desire for greater observance of asceticism, poverty, and regularity, but also to avoid the burden of educational work. There were, however, some exceptions, and from the second half of the twelfth century we have some cases of children being accepted.[5] And in the traditional monasteries parents were tending to offer their children less frequently, some even attempting to prevent their sons and daughters from entering monastic life. It is during this period that we see two contrary types of literature appearing. There was both propaganda against the monastic vocation and the fact of becoming a monk, and also letters written by monks to men who were once their companions in the schools or in knighthood urging them to enter monastic life and thus taste the happiness of the paradise of the cloister.[6]

At this same period, the canonists affirmed that young adults had the right to decide freely as to their own future, either in marriage or in the monastic state.[7] Entrance into the monastery thus gradually became more and more of a personal and free choice, which accounts for a fact that had so far been unknown: the majority of the new orders recruited their members from among adults.

These adults came from different social categories. Many were said to be 'nobles' or 'knights'. The difficulty of discerning with any precision the exact meaning of the words *nobiles* and *milites* is well known.[8] In the course of the twelfth century the idea and the reality expressed by 'nobility' became more precise and more diversified. Such evolution took place at a different pace in different countries and areas. In general, the process entailed a progression from knighthood—*militia*, cavalry: a warrior and usually a mounted warrior—to feudalism, that is to personal dependence based on faith or fealty, and then to nobility, which was an honour bestowed for the accomplishment of these offices. Briefly, we may say that in some cases there was progression from cavalry to chivalry. Among those adults who entered monasteries, some were both knights and nobles—belonging to the higher or lower nobility—and others were knights but not noblemen. However, all had previously lived in castles or other types of manors, dwellings proper to the aristocracy as a whole; some had even lived at courts.[9]

Other members of the new orders had formerly been students in the city schools which had been set up in contradistinction to the monastic schools. Thus in the twelfth century the word *scholaris*, though it still designated the monastic oblates, also came gradually to mean the students in urban schools.[10] Such were those young nobles from Carinthia, some of whom were related to the emperor, who, on their way back from the schools in Paris, put up at the guest-house of Morimond in Lotharingia not far from Clairvaux and stayed on to enter the noviciate. After monastic profession, they returned to their own countries to found monasteries. Such recruits were 'clerics', but their vocation is described in military terms: the abbey of Morimond is called a watch-tower, where combat is waged against the devil.[11] In other cases of adult recruitment, the noblemen and ladies who entered were widowers and widows. Others, again, purely and simply left their wives or husbands to come to the monastery. Married couples sometimes entered double monasteries with their children. Recent statistics of recruitment of nunneries in Western France during the twelfth century show that between 21 and 52 per cent of the nuns had been married.[12] Needless to say, this general sketch of trends in new recruitment requires more detailed development, and there are documents which would allow of this, yet even so we can already see from this outline that these new recruits to the new orders were different from members of the traditional monasteries, in that *they all had lived in secular society*.

II. *Psychological implications*

The psychological implications of this fact are well illustrated by a passage from St. Bernard's address to his monks in his second Sermon on the Dedication of the Church of Clairvaux:

Do you wish me to give you a proof of the sanctity of those I am speaking of and to show you the miracles of the saints among us? Why, there are many among you who, after having rotted away in their sins and vices like barn animals in their dung, and having had the courage to leave them behind, continue to resist their daily attacks, as the Apostle says when speaking of the saints: 'They have recovered from their sickness and have become strong in combat.' What could be more marvellous than a person who formerly could hardly abstain three days from lust, gluttony, revelling, drunkenness, debauchery, and impurity, as well as a hundred other vices, whatever they may be, and yet who now abstains from them for years at a time, even for a whole lifetime? What could be a greater miracle than so many young people, *iuvenes*, so many youths and nobles, *nobiles*, all those, in short, whom I see here, remaining, so to speak, in an open prison, being bound by the fear of God alone and persevering in hard penance, something which is in my eyes beyond human power, above human nature, and which goes very much against the grain.[13]

Finally, in the field of monastic sociology, there is another fact which cannot be overlooked: namely the rise of a new image of the nun. This began with Robert of Arbrissel (1050-1117), who lived and wrote during the same period and in the same area as William IX of Aquitaine and was contemporary with the first troubadours. Under his influence a great number of women withdrew from secular society. These women were often young and beautiful; many were noble ladies, others belonged to the other various levels of society. These nunneries were often served by monasteries of monks under the government of a lady abbess. Fifty years after its foundation, Robert of Arbrissel's order counted four or five thousand members, living out in several dozen houses. Such was the first and most famous example of a whole new trend which developed in the twelfth century. Robert's biographer, Baudry of Dole, tells us that at Fontevrault there was an influx 'of men of every state, women both poor and noble, virgins and widows, elderly and young, prostitutes and those who had never known man'. There, as at Cîteaux, Clair-vaux, and in the early Church, charity was the source of mutual understanding. Such a group needed to be organized. The founder preferred to name widows as superiors rather than young, inexperienced girls. The recruits were lodged in adjacent buildings: the virgins and the widows, the sick, the lepers, the repentant prostitutes, and then the monks charged with the celebration of worship or manual labour in the service of the nuns. Neither the incestuous nor the handicapped were excluded. These different categories were separated materially for reasons of prudence, but they were spiritually united: 'there was no discord, neither in their intentions, nor in their acts'.[14] As usually happens, such descriptions of nascent congregations are probably idealized: nevertheless, they are revealing of the Utopian goal: a society united in love for God, love which over-rode all social barriers of secular society.

In the next generation, we have a singular illustration of this feminine promotion in a nun, both an abbess and a writer who corresponded with St. Bernard and was considered to be a prophetess: St. Hildegard. Though she still justified the exist-ence of noble monasteries,[15] she produced, among her various encyclopedic works, poems and other writings in which she expressed a typically feminine form of love which would merit careful study by women psychologists—or at least with their help! She is the first of many women who wrote about love.

We are now in a position to study the psychological implications of the sociological changes connected with the new recruitment, especially as reflected in monastic love literature.

The first obvious fact is that many of these monks and nuns came to monasteries with definite knowledge of secular love. This they had acquired either from experience—within the married state or outside of it—or from the reading of love literature. It would therefore seem quite lawful to wonder whether there were not some relation between the fact that, firstly, it was mainly, almost exclusively, in the new orders that monastic love literature was produced in the twelfth century, and, secondly, it was also the new orders which, with adult recruitment, accepted troubadours and trouvères. This was particularly true of Cîteaux. One of the most illustrious examples is Helinand, one-time trouvère at the court of Philip Augustus, who entered at Froidmont, where he continued to write prose and verse. There was also the troubadour Folquet who, among his many works, wrote fourteen love songs. He entered Thoronet in 1196, became abbot five years later, and was named bishop of Marseilles in 1203. We read that 'one day he fasted on bread and water, in a spirit of penance, after hearing a song he had composed in his former life'.[16] After his death the Cistercians commemorated him as a saint, and Dante in his *Paradiso* set him in the heaven of Venus.[17] These two very different honours both became him, and it was fitting that he should have been given them.

There is another thing to be noticed, and this has only recently been pointed out. It is remarkable that the feminine is almost absent from Peter the Venerable's marvellous accounts of Cluny, whereas in Cistercian writings of the same genre it is very definitely present, and there is even a certain charm and tenderness. The Cistercian descriptions are not restricted to visual images of the Blessed Virgin. There is also mention of beautiful, delightful young maidens and, here and there, we notice hints about their loving caresses and kisses. The kisses are, of course, chaste, but even so they call forth a defensive reaction from monks who, on waking up, realize what they have been dreaming about. This suggests that such men are sensitive to these nocturnal visions, which recall sexual or literary experiences graved in the memory.[18]

Adult recruitment as practised by the new orders fostered the development of two new categories of writings. One of these was made up of treatises dealing with the formation of novices.[19] It is easy to understand that new methods were necessary if adults were to adapt to monastic life. Children who entered were trained in monastic ways from their early years, whereas a double process was required in the training of adults: there had to be a preliminary psychological and spiritual destructuring before the new monastic structure could be erected. The radical change in the scale of values implied for an adult man or woman coming to monastic life is much more difficult than for children. It is also a more conscious and freely assumed process. Stephen of Salley, for example, in his *Mirror for Novices*, makes a very precise allusion to the memories left by former worldly living on a man's psycho-dynamics, which need to be transformed.[20]

The second new group of writings is that on monastic love. Such literature already existed, but it became more abundant and profuse with the expansion of the new orders. Without this literature, traditional monasticism would not have survived. Nor would it have paved the way for the twelfth-century renewal. But before this period it dwelt mainly on charity as being a virtue among others. Writings on love were incorporated into works on the Christian mystery. Love as charity was the object of sermons, prayers, hymns. It was a virtue to be practised, and the *Lives* of the Saints proposed examples. In the new monasticism, however, teaching on love became much more explicit, and the love for God and men was expounded upon in many love texts. The herald of this new doctrine on love was love's first poet and theologian: Bernard of Clairvaux. Before being abbot of Clairvaux, and the greatest monastic author of the twelfth century, he was the dutiful son of a knight and a humble monk of Cîteaux. He was an extraordinary recruit, indeed, and one who is of special interest in that his writings reveal not only his own adult psychology but also that of his audience, made up of adult recruits. It is worth spending a little time on this unpredictable newcomer.

III. *The unpredictable St. Bernard*

The pivot of all monastic love literature in the twelfth century was the conversion, work, and influence of Bernard of Clairvaux. Born in 1090, he entered the noviciate of Cîteaux twenty-two years later. He arrived with a group of young knights who had been literally conquered by him, and the changes which occurred from then onward were hinged on his dynamic personality. When did he first start writing about love? William of Saint-Thierry in his *Vita Prima* and other official biographers are silent on that point.[21] But the *Vita Prima* was written as support for canonization, so that it is a no more reliable source than the other works. All are constructed round the traditional hagiographical commonplaces, and offer no proof that Bernard in his adolescence suffered from an overstrong repression accounting for equally unbalanced aggression in everything he did in his more mature years. The truth, as witnessed to by facts of any historical veracity, would seem to be rather that Bernard as a young man was psychologically sound: he was normally sensitive to pleasure but always self-controlled.[22] In the first book of the *Vita Prima* written by William of Saint-Thierry we do detect a certain strong emotional stress and other psychological problems, but these are more revealing of William's psyche than of Bernard's. However, it might be possible to apply to St. Bernard a suggestion made by the author of a penetrating study on the temptation and conflict suffered by St. Benedict as described by St. Gregory the Great. The author of this study writes:

Thus, anger, when controlled, becomes the vehicle of good zeal; pride brought low can be pressed into service in defence of justice. . . . If a strong sexuality is brought under control and disciplined by the practice of works of mercy, the very quarter whence people are exposed to the darts of wickedness becomes itself an incitement to solicitude for others.[23]

If the application of these words to St. Bernard is apposite, then it might well be accordingly inferred that when he was a young man he heroically rode a great storm and came through victorious, and consequently his charisma as a leader was served by sublimated emotionality. Any such considerations are based, not on historical evidence, but on psychological deductions. Other texts seem to show that Bernard was not inhibited or repressed in his spontaneous needs and even that he kept his unsuppressed drives under control with some success.[24]

This is all we can deduce about Bernard's adolescence. Do we know any more about his youth before he came to Cîteaux? In particular, can we say for sure when he began to write spiritual works? Were these his first writings? On this subject there is one text worth examining. Many years later, in an apology in favour of Abelard, a certain Berengar brought forward accusations against Bernard. The exact sense of these is difficult to grasp through the medium of a conventional and imprecise Latin vocabulary: moreover, it is not even certain that the text we have is accurate.[25] In it Berengar criticizes Bernard's abundant eloquence (*ubertatem facundiae*), remarking that it is not astonishing: 'Quite the contrary, it would be astonishing were your language to be dry and arid, for we have heard it said that from the beginning of your adolescence (*a primis fere adolescentiae rudimentis*), you used to write mocking and alluring tunes and profane melodies (*cantiunculas mimicas et urbanos modulos fictitasse*). And this is no hesitant opinion on my part, for your country itself, which became your student, witnesses in favour of what I have said (*testis est alumna tui patria nostri sermonis*). Is it not stamped deep down in your memory (*nonne id etiam tuae memoriae altius est insignitum*) that in competitions of rhymed verse you strove always to outdo your brothers by your facility, ability, agility for inventions (*fratres tuos rhythmico certamine*

acutaeque inventionis versutia semper exsuperare contendebas), and
it seemed a very keen insult to you that one of them answered
back with as much impudence (*pari responderet protervia*). In the
present work I could, on the testimony of witnesses worthy of
belief, insert some of your nonsenses (*aliqua de nugis tuis*), but in
so doing I would fear to sully my own work. Moreover, a universally known fact has no need of witnesses. And now you
often use in the service of God your habit of composing fictions
and fooleries (*illum itaque commentandi et nugendi usum*).'

This text calls for several remarks. Firstly, it is not at all
impossible that in his youth Bernard composed frivolous songs,
in the company of his brothers and men like them: his five
brothers were among those hot-headed and idle sons of knights
who spent their time leading the easy-going life of a castle in a
small Burgundian court, and sparring in the neighbourhood.

Furthermore, Berengar's witness is the only one of its kind:
no one else has written in the same vein. Moreover, it is in such
a partial, passionate, hate-filled, and exaggerated context that
it is extremely suspect. Professor David Luscombe, who has
dealt with what Berengar had to say against St. Bernard on the
occasion of the Council of Sens, has come to the conclusion
that his criticism has no historical value. Berengar, he writes,
is 'too temperamental', he allowed his passion to outweigh
his judgement; at times 'he descends to the lowest depth of
absurdity'.[26]

What Berengar affirms in the fragment of text under analysis
is contradicted by information from other sources about the
Council of Sens held in 1140, as well as by the popularity of
Bernard's *Sermons on the Song of Songs*, which, according to
Berengar, are devoid of value and not worth reading. In fact, his
invective aroused such indignation that he had to excuse himself in another writing which we shall presently quote. There is
no extant copy of any poem similar to those Bernard is accused of
composing, but they may have existed at the time of his entry
at Cîteaux, since Berengar himself had some in his possession
and supposed that they were fairly widely diffused, if, as he

affirmed, they were universally known. However, it may be
that some have been preserved and not yet discovered, or
perhaps attributed to some anonymous writer. Of the sacred
poems certainly written by Bernard, we have only the hymn of
his *Office of St. Victor*, and a hymn and an epitaph in honour of
St. Malachy.[27] And it is true that Bernard would have been able
to compose many more sacred poems: many of his passages are
real poems in prose, and they contain phrases which could be
set out in the form of verse, with rhythm and rhyme;[28] A. Dimier,
in fact, has given to the first essay written on this subject the
characteristic title: *Les amusements poétiques de St. Bernard*,
poetical entertainments of St. Bernard.[29]

Lastly, the terms in which Berengar describes the songs
Bernard wrote in his youth never mention clearly that they were
erotic: he mentions nonsense, trifling talk (what we today would
call 'jokes'), and a certain facility for composing light verse,
frivolous tunes. All this is in accordance with Bernard's fluency
of style, which he maintained later in his spiritual works. On
this point, literary criticism shows Berengar to be right, because
Bernard does excel in play of words—both in sound and in
meaning—in all those entertaining tricks and puns which go
to make some of his writing into a literary firework display.[30]
But we may well suppose that had Berengar found matter for
making definite accusations in the sphere of moral behaviour,
he would have done so.

As we have already said, the *Apologia* written by Berengar was
found to be so unjust that its author, in a *Letter to the Bishop
of Mende* several years later, thought it necessary to make
reparation.[31] He acknowledges the holiness of the abbot of
Clairvaux, which has put him beyond the reach of human
opinion, without, however, its implying that he ceases to be a
man: 'Is the abbot of Clairvaux not a man?' There were storms
in him as in every other man; there is something sublime in him
and something quite the opposite. 'He is the Martin of our
times': he is a light, but in a lantern. In short, Berengar excuses
himself, but does not retract what he once wrote: 'Let those

who are informed read my *Apologia*, and if I have made unjust reproaches about this abbot, they have every right to refute them.' But he carefully avoids going further into detail, particularly with regard to Bernard's youthful songs, which are perhaps simply hinted at by this allusion: 'If then the abbot wrote certain things which ought not to be spoken of, how has truth sinned by my mouth when she declared that they ought to be done away with?' This applies to the general criticism he had made of Bernard's style as a whole—a point on which future generations disagreed with him—and not to the poems for which he had reproached him.

And what is his witness on these poems worth? In his letter he acknowledges that when Abelard was condemned, in 1140, he himself was a beardless adolescent, still at an age for doing declensions in school: had he already heard about the songs which Bernard composed more than thirty years earlier, before his conversion in 1111? As to the witnesses called upon by Berengar, there is some obscurity. Would it be that Bernard's own brothers, long after they had become monks, had spoken to him about their brother's youthful levity? All that is hardly likely, and we are obliged to conclude that it remains open to question whether or not Bernard once wrote poems of secular love: so many people wrote love songs in those days.

William of Saint-Thierry states—and on this point we may believe him—that the young man Bernard, after his conversion, when he spoke in favour of the monastic life, had a real gift for seducing people: 'Mothers hid their sons and wives their husbands, friends prevented him from meeting their friends, for the Holy Spirit gave such efficacy to his voice, that only the strongest antipathy could resist him.'[32] This seducer for God could well have been, before his conversion, seducing for another love, and, were that true, it would only serve to stress the seriousness of his conversion.

Bernard belonged to a family of noble knights, though he himself was not of the highest ranks of nobility. Had knighthood actually been conferred on him? It seems probable that if it had been, then either he or his biographers, or his admirers, perhaps his few enemies, would have made allusion to this. What is certain is that he helped to create, in the Knightly Order of the Templars, whose founder and first Master was his own cousin, Hugh of Payns, a monastic nobility, parallel to secular aristocracy. His purpose, when writing his treatise *In Praise of the New Militia; to the Knights of the Temple*,[33] was not so much to propagate interest in a nascent institution which was still frail and which mainly recruited from the lower nobility, as to find expression for his own ideal of knighthood. There he made room for the ideal of martyrdom which the *Chanson de Roland* and other chansons de geste and romances on the crusades had brought to a logical conclusion when applied to some of their heroes. Bernard wrote a strong criticism of secular knighthood also, which may appear to be exaggerated satire, but which has been justified by the no less violent portrait of the knights found in a text recently published by Marvin L. Colker in his *Analecta Dublinensia*.[34] Between the ideal of knighthood and its reality, there was an enormous gap. Bernard did not have to Christianize knighthood: this had already been attempted before him. But he did try to reform it, just as he tried to reform all the other institutions of his times.

What is apparent from his and other contemporary witnesses is that knighthood favoured violence, pride, vanity, and sensuality. We understand why Bernard not only helped to create a parallel knighthood of soldier monks in the Order of the Temple, but also recruited a vast 'peace corps', made up of several thousand monks whom he drew away from knighthood and nobility to fill the several hundred monasteries which he founded or helped to develop in the Cistercian and other new orders.[35] It was to these former knights become monks that he addressed his daily sermons, adapting his manner of preaching to their psychology.

In the circles of knighthood and nobility, love literature had begun to flourish, and Bernard could hardly fail to determine to create a corresponding love literature, which he did with steady

continuity. And it is these writings which are his specific
contribution to monastic spiritual culture.

In 1124 or 1125 Bernard wrote a long letter on the love of
God, the eleventh in the corpus; it is so important and so
beautiful that an attempt has been made to prove that it was the
'first letter' written by him.[36] Whether or not this is correct, it
is the first to be developed in the form of a theoretical treatise.
The famous 'letter to Robert', which was his first manifesto in
favour of Cistercian life, was only dictated at a later date. From
then on Bernard never ceased writing about love: between 1126
and 1141 he composed the treatise *On the Necessity of Loving
God*;[37] from 1135 onwards he began a long commentary on the
love poem which is the Song of Songs, on which he worked for
eighteen years, and which death prevented him from complet-
ing.[38] Now, in all these works he did no more than expand the
teaching already contained in the basic Letter 11, which he
himself considered to be so fundamental that he reproduced it,
without the slightest modification, at the end of his treatise on
the love of God.[39] This text was the fruit of fifteen years of
monastic ripening, and of some former experience which is
unknown to us. Early as it is, this work is a dense, lucid, poetical,
and theological praise of disinterested love, one which is pure,
'chaste, filial, stainless', for God and man; it is *the* decisive
manifesto on monastic love in the twelfth century. All that was
to be written on the subject in future years, either by Bernard
himself or by his friends and disciples such as William of Saint-
Thierry and Aelred of Rievaulx, by those who imitated and
developed his *Sermons on the Song*, followed in the wake of this
first document. It is here and nowhere else, whatever the former
experience may have been that helped him to arrive at this point,
that Bernard gives the lead and sets the tone for all that was to
influence future love literature in monastic society. What strikes
one as remarkable is that Bernard never says or assumes that the
love which tends to union with God excludes an accompanying
love tending to union between human persons, which remains
within what he calls the order of charity, or 'charity in order'.

Monastic love and other forms of Christian love have a different quality, but the latter can and ought to be integrated into this love for God. And monastic love for God can and must be expressed in terms of human love; it can assume, retrieve, and integrate images, representations of human love, and even memories of its accomplishment, as seems to have been the case with some young men who had become monks. It is also possible to show that the deep and spontaneous attitude to femininity and women was much more positive in Bernard and in members of the new orders than it had been, and continued to be, in representatives of traditional monasticism. The same love for God diffuses itself equally to all men and women, even if, in order to be conserved in its integrity by people voluntarily vowed to celibacy, it necessitates a certain distance, a reserve, between men and women: nevertheless, love for God is often, and preferentially, symbolized by love between a man and a woman.

The difference of psyche between people in the world and those in the cloister—all coming from a society with the same social barriers—does not arise from the difference of social levels, but of states of life: secular and monastic. In monastic love the structures of secular society are overcome, though not always ignored: monks and nuns entering the cloister now as adults knew about secular love, from books or experience, but were governed by love for God and therefore tended to express this love towards other human beings.

And it is understandable that the only way for human beings to overcome the barriers that distinguish, separate, and sometimes bitterly divide them, is for all to love, first and foremost, a Being who is unlimited by these differences, but whose love—that is to say—whose presence, allows of conciliation, and if necessary, reconciliation. In short, the only love which in the twelfth century was able to overcome, though not always perfectly nor without difficulty, social barriers, is the one taught, learned, and practised in the cloisters, each one of which was supposed to be a *schola caritatis*, a school of charity.

¹ J. H. Lynch, 'Monastic Recruitment in the Eleventh and Twelfth Centuries: Some Social and Economic Considerations', *American Benedictine Review*, 26 (1975), pp. 425–47; and *Simoniacal Entry into Religious Life from 1000 to 1260. A Social, Economic and Legal Study*, Ohio State University Press, Columbus, 1976, pp. 36–60.

² Facts, texts, and references are to be found in the article 'Nobiltà', forthcoming in the *Dizionario degli Istituti di Perfezione*, VI, Rome, 1979, forthcoming.

³ The life of Herman the Counterfeit (1013–54), a monk of Reichenau, and the description of his 'paralising pain' are in *P.L.* 143. 25–30. Other details on his illness are given in a text published by R. B. C. Huygens, 'Deux commentaires sur la séquence "Ave praeclara maris stella"', *Cîteaux*, 20 (1969), pp. 113 and 128.

⁴ Literature has very few texts on the unhappy nun; P. Dronke, *Medieval Latin and the Rise of European Love-Lyric*, Oxford, 1968, pp. 353–60, has published and commented on two of them, vol. II, pp. 353–60; cf. vol. I, pp. 221–39: 'Convents and "courtoisie"'. For what concerns the pedagogy exercised on children destined to become monks and the marks it left on them when they were grown-up, the documents are to be used with some precaution: people without problems do not usually write. M. M. McLaughlin has pointed out this difficulty in the interpretation of the sources, and collated witnesses in: 'Survivors and Surrogates: Children and Parents from the Ninth to the Thirteenth Century', in *The History of Childhood*, ed. Lloyd deMause, New York, 1974, pp. 129–32; also P. Riché, 'L'enfant dans la société monastique au XIIᵉ siècle', in *Pierre Abélard-Pierre le Vénérable. Les courants philosophiques, littéraires et artistiques en Occident au milieu du XIIᵉ siècle*, Paris, 1975, pp. 689–701. J. F. Benton has written that 'nuns and monks seem to be the best parents in the early Middle Ages', 'Individualism and Conformity in Medieval Western Europe', in *Fifth Giorgio della Vida Biennial Conference. Individualism and Conformity in Classical Islam*, Wiesbaden, 1977, p. 156.

⁵ J. H. Lynch, 'The Cistercians and underage Novices', *Cîteaux*, 24 (1973), pp. 283–97. Other witnesses could be added.

⁶ On all these points: 'Textes sur la vocation et la formation des moines au moyen âge', in *Corona gratiarum. Miscellanea . . . Eligio Dekkers . . . oblata*, II, Bruges-The Hague, 1975, pp. 169–94.

⁷ Article 'Noviziato', in *Dizionario degli Istituti di Perfezione*, VI, Rome, 1979, forthcoming.

⁸ Let it suffice to refer, by way of example, to the recent works of J. Flori: 'La notion de chevalerie dans les chansons de geste du XIIᵉ siècle', *Le moyen âge*, 81 (1975), pp. 211–44 and 407–45; 'Sémantique et société médiévale. Le verbe "adouber" et son évolution au XIIᵉ siècle', *Annales E.S.C.* 31 (1976), pp. 915–40; 'Chevaliers et chevalerie au XIᵉ siècle en France et dans l'Empire germanique à propos d'un livre récent', *Le moyen âge*, 82 (1976), pp. 125–36.

⁹ Witness to this is seen, for example, in the texts quoted by A. Chèvre, *Lucelle. Histoire d'une ancienne abbaye cistercienne*, Delémont, 1975, pp. 44–66; J. Legendre, *La Chartreuse de Lugny des origines au début du XIVᵉ siècle. 1172–1332*, Salzburg, 1975, pp. 155–72; J. B. Freed, 'Urban Development and the "cura monialum" in Twentieth Century Germany', *Viator*, 3 (1972), pp. 316–23; and earlier on, A. Dimier, *S. Bernard, pêcheur de Dieu*, Paris, 1953, pp. 56 and 173–95; 'Les captures de S. Bernard aux Pays-Bas. La chapelle des comtes de Flandres à Clairvaux', in *Comité Flamand de France*, Lille, 1954, pp. 80 and 82.

¹⁰ 'The Growth of the Critical Attitude of Students towards the Masters', forthcoming in the *Proceedings of the Colloquium of Comparative Church History* (British Sub-Commission), Oxford, 1974.

¹¹ The text is in the 'Continuatio Claustroneoburgensis I', in *MGH, SS* 9, p. 610; the account is commented on by L. Grill, in the collective work, *Bernard de*

Clairvaux, Paris, 1953, pp. 143-4 (on other noblemen who became Cistercians, ibid., pp. 138-42).

[12] J. Verdon, 'Les moniales dans l'Ouest de la France aux XIe et XIIe siècles. Étude d'histoire sociale', *Cahiers de civilisation médiévale*, 19 (1976), pp. 247-64. The first condition for dissolution of marriage was an 'honest agreement', as wrote, for example, in 1133-5, a certain William (whom some have thought to be William of Saint-Thierry) in a debate with Henry of Lausanne. The text is translated in R. I. Moore, *The Birth of Popular Heresy*, London, 1975, p. 54.

[13] 'Sermo in Dedicatione ecclesiae', I. 2, *S. Bernardi opera*, V, Rome, 1968, p. 371. In the rest of these sermons on the dedication, the vocabulary of the *militia* is used frequently and with precision: monks are said to be the *ministeriales* of God, the monastic life entails a combat (*bellum, militia*), the monastery is compared to a fortress with all that goes to make it up: *murus, antemurale, castrum, armatura*, etc.

[14] *Vita B. Roberti de Arbrisello*, n. 19, 24, *P.L.* 162. 1053-6.

[15] *Scivias*, II. 5, *P.L.* 197. 500-2.

[16] According to Robert de Sorbon, cited by S. Stronski, *Le troubadour Folquet de Marseille*, Cracow, 1910, p. 112^x; B. Bulton, 'Fulk of Toulouse: the Escape that Failed', in *Church, Society and Politics. Studies in Church History*, 12 (1975), ed. D. Baker, p. 90, suggests that the reason why Fulk protested was that they tried to flatter him by singing one of his own poems to him.

[17] *Par.* IX. 64-108.

[18] Texts and facts are quoted, in this sense, by D. Bouthillier, 'L'univers religieux de Pierre le Vénérable d'après le "De miraculis" à la lumière des autres œuvres de l'auteur et de la tradition bénédictine et cistercienne', mimeographed thesis, Montreal, 1975, pp. 409-11.

[19] References in 'Textes sur la vocation', loc. cit., p. 184.

[20] Ed. E. Mikkers, 'Un "Speculum novitii" inédit d'Etienne de Salley', in *Collectanea Ord. Cist. Ref.* 8 (1946), p. 45. 16-17.

[21] 'Le premier biographe de S. Bernard', in *Nouveau visage de Bernard de Clairvaux. Approches psycho-historiques*, Paris, 1976, pp. 11-34.

[22] 'Agressivité et répression chez Bernard de Clairvaux', *Revue d'histoire de la spiritualité*, 52 (1976), pp. 155-72.

[23] P. A. Cusack, 'The Temptation of St. Benedict: An Essay at Interpretation through the Literary Sources', *American Benedictine Review*, 27 (1976), p. 162.

[24] *Nouveau visage de Bernard de Clairvaux*, pp. 52-8 and *passim*.

[25] *Liber Apologeticus*, *P.L.* 178. 1857.

[26] 'Berengar, Defender of Abelard', *Recherches de théologie ancienne et médiévale*, 33 (1966), p. 336.

[27] Ed. *S. Bernardi opera*, III, Rome, 1963, pp. 517-26.

[28] *Recueil d'études sur S. Bernard*, III, Rome, 1969, pp. 180-208, and other studies in vol. IV of the same work (Rome, 1978, forthcoming).

[29] *Collectanea Ord. Cist. Ref.* 11 (1949), pp. 53-5.

[30] Bernard's ability to play with words, his playfulness, suggested a certain kinship between him and Mozart: *Recueil d'études*, III, pp. 205-10.

[31] *P.L.* 178. 1871-2.

[32] *Vita prima*, I. 15, *P.L.* 185. 235.

[33] *S. Bernardi opera*, III, pp. 213-39.

[34] M. L. Colker, *Analecta Dublinensia. Three Medieval Latin Texts in the Library of Trinity College, Dublin*, Cambridge, 1976.

[35] 'Saint Bernard's Attitude Towards War', in *Studies in Medieval Cistercian History*, II, ed. J. R. Sommerfeldt, Kalamazoo, 1976, pp. 2-13. In the same sense, K. Bertau, *Deutsche Literatur im Europäischen Mittelalter*, Munich, 1973, pp. 108-11.

[36] Ed. *S. Bernardi opera*, VII, Rome, 1974, pp. 52-60. The final touches which Bernard made on this letter in his last edition (P) compared with the texts of the two preceding editions (B and L), as they are shown by the critical apparatus are minor. Contrary to certain of Bernard's other works, the primitive text of Letter 11 was neither greatly modified, nor lengthened, neither in the two following drafts of it, nor in the *De diligendo Deo*. For the date, see D. van den Eynde, in *Recueil d'études sur S. Bernard*, III, p. 356. The hypothesis according to which Letter 11 was Bernard's first letter was put forth by L. Grill, 'Epistola de Caritate: der älteste St. Bernhards-Brief', *Cîteaux*, 15 (1964), pp. 26-51.

[37] *S. Bernardi opera*, III, p. 111.

[38] On this chronology, *Recueil d'études*, I, Rome, 1962, pp. 233-43.

[39] *S. Bernardi opera*, III, pp. 148-54.

III

A Biblical Master of Love: Solomon

THE complex and vast literature on love, within monasticism and among seculars, is bound to have many and varied sources; there is no question of dealing with all these here at any depth and even less with originality. The most we can do is to give the characteristics of the more important literary sources and endeavour to evaluate the peculiar influence of each. By far the most important doctrinal source, not only for what concerns monastic love literature in particular, but also for literature in general concerning love, since it too appears in a Christian milieu, is the New Testament. Its ideas are to be found everywhere, more or less diffusely, as in all other Christian writings. But since we are dealing with works whose specific theme is love itself, we must expect to find that the authors who had the most direct influence are those who spoke more particularly on this subject. There are two who call for special mention: Solomon and Ovid. Both these names should be put into inverted commas and in the plural, because we are dealing not with the Solomon and Ovid who lived in history, but with the Solomon and Ovid who lived in the minds of twelfth-century people, especially monks; furthermore, each of these names denoted various historical and non-historical, therefore symbolic, authors and models.

I. *The Solomon of the Song of Songs, and others*

From the eleventh century onwards the manuscripts of Ovid increased in number, and that began what has been called the *aetas Ovidiana*. We could say there was also an *aetas*

Salomoniana, though here we must understand the reality behind the name. We may say that several Solomons were known in those days. There was the historical Solomon whose life and adventures are set forth in the Book of Kings and who fell victim to his fleshly lusts; 'He loved many foreign women. . . . He clung to these in love. . . . He had several hundred wives, princesses, and three hundred concubines . . .' (I Kings 11: 1–3). Then there was the philosopher Solomon to whom were attributed the Sapiential Books, in which every reader could find something to his taste. There was the erotic Solomon, some of whose statements might well have been read in Ovid: 'Whatever my eyes desired I did not keep from them; I kept my heart from no pleasure . . .' (Eccles. 2: 10). Again, there is the moralizing Solomon: 'I loved wisdom more than health and beauty' (Wisd. 7: 10). 'I loved her and sought her from my youth and I desired to take her for my bride . . .' (8: 2); 'in friendship with her, pure delight . . .' (8: 18). Solomon the sage was also a master in the making of proverbs, parables, and every sort of poem. From all the different writings in his name it was possible to draw precepts and beautiful formulas for embellishing one's own style. There are specific passages, as in Ovid, which acted rather as an antidote to love, in which woman is far from idealized, as in this tirade found in Sirach:

> Do not look upon one for beauty,
> and do not sit in the midst of women;
> for from garments come the moths,
> and from a woman comes woman's wickedness.
> Better is the wickedness of a man
> than a woman who does good:
> and it is the woman who brings shame and disgrace.[1]

However, all these different Solomons—the historical, erotic, philosophical, or lettered one—are far less quoted and have less influence on the mentality of the various authors and their writings than does the mystical Solomon to whom the Song of Songs is attributed. Now, is the author of this book to be described as mystical or erotic? That is a problem for the

specialists in biblical literature to fight out. And it did occasionally happen in the middle ages, though rarely, and only in later
periods, for one or other formula from the Song of Songs to be
used in erotic contexts. For monastic and secular literature on
the whole, we can apply with some reservations this observation
made by Edmond Faral, a historian who is as competent as he is
impartial: 'It is remarkable that the Song of Songs, the reading
of which could awaken, from some aspects, profane curiosity,
has never been interpreted, in the many commentaries written
from the tenth to the fourteenth century, otherwise than in the
sense of religious sentiments and mysticism. No lay author ever
saw in it, for his inspiration, any signs of human passion.'[2] So,
when the Song of Songs becomes something more than a
beautiful lyric to serve as a source of inspiration, it is always in
connection with love, and a 'monastic' sort of love. Thus, in
keeping with this tradition, the Solomon to whom this work is
attributed has rightly been described as a man who 'teaches—
docet—love of God alone'.[3] This is certainly the 'doctor' who
has left the greatest impression on the first love literature in
twelfth-century France, that is to say, monastic love literature,
therefore it is his influence which must be analysed in the first
place.

II. *A symbolic tradition*

The interpretation to be given to the Song of Songs has long
aroused among specialists in Holy Scripture a controversy which
does not seem to be abating in the least.[4] Some of these scholars
see in the text a purely allegorical song, where the images
borrowed from human love are symbols evoking the relationship between God and his people Israel, or else the Holy City,
Jerusalem, or again the Temple, the Church, the Virgin Mary,
the Christian soul;[5] whereas others say it is nothing more than
a love poem, and some even go so far as to say it is an erotic poem.
One of the biblical scholars who has recently and most radically
analysed the Song in this way is a very competent German
Benedictine monk, who, after having published many learned

philological and theological works on the Song, acknowledges that he has gone through a sort of conversion process because of his recent discovery of C. Jung: and now everything can be explained, so he says, by means of schemas borrowed from this psychologist.[6] Naturally, between these two extremes, there are also moderate interpretations, which endeavour to reconcile elements taken from the two.

One would need to have the competence of an expert in the matter in order to take part in any such discussion and judge objectively the arguments put forth on the one hand or the other, but it is at least clear that the Song of Songs can be read in very different ways. In fact, it has been used symbolically in various ways perhaps by the authors of the New Testament, surely by the Fathers of the Church, monastic writers, and the compilers of the Targums—that is to say paraphrases—in ancient and medieval Judaism. This particular tradition has always been universally homogeneous, but especially so in Champagne and particularly at Troyes, not far from the Abbey of Clairvaux. It was there that the famous Rabbi Rashi taught and wrote, and, either through his own writings or else through the medium of his disciples, he influenced Peter Comestor, a contemporary of St. Bernard and Dean of Troyes Cathedral from 1147 to 1165.[7] Now, all the medieval rabbinic commentaries commonly gave an allegorical interpretation to the Song. There is only one exception to this, and it is from a later commentary, for it was put forth by a 'French rabbi of the northern school who without any doubt lived in the thirteenth century'.[8] This author sees the biblical book of the Song as nothing more than an erotic poem, and 'from this point of view, it seems to be the only one of its kind among the commentaries which have come down to us'.[9]

Today, according to the school of literature, psychology, psycho-analysis, structuralism, or socio-cultural history to which we might belong, we can, as it were, ask for the key to interpretation from Freud, Jung, Alder, Lacan, and many others. Thus we may not exclude the possibility that any similar problem could have existed in religious literature in the high middle ages. But, actually, such a problem does not appear to have existed and this is one of the major arguments pointing to the homogeneity of a culture prevalent in a long series of centuries throughout the whole of Western Christianity. The people went through very many changes and evolutions and sometimes there were profound transformations in the social, economic, political, scientific, psychological, and many other spheres. But in the field of religious culture, and in any case in monastic milieux, we notice a remarkable continuity and unanimity. On the very point with which we are dealing here, this is shown by the interpretation given to the Song: it was symbolical and not erotic. This is to be explained by obvious reasons. First of all, the vocabulary and even the notion of love are fundamental to Christianity: they express its very essence: 'God is love', as says the definition given by the First Epistle of St. John (4: 8); thus any relationship to God can only be a relationship of love, and we notice that it is evoked as such in many texts.

But the language and symbolism of love apply also—and first of all—to the relations between human persons. Thus it is normal that there should be an easy and even quite natural shift from one level of the representation of love to the other. To the long period between John the Evangelist and John of the Cross we can apply what has been written about the latter: 'The symbols of the manifestation of love are evidently referred to erotic activity: this does not necessarily mean that spiritual love must be reduced to carnal love. It would be naïve to try to deny the connections and the possible contaminations between the two levels: but it would be vulgar to reduce the higher one to the lower.'[10]

The analogy of human love had moreover always been used by biblical writers before the New Testament. There was, then, a very ancient tradition, and this could not fail to mark deeply the readers and commentators of the Bible as a whole, and of the Song of Songs in particular.

But besides this important fact, there is another one which is proper to the Greek and Latin traditions and to those which later were dependent on them. A North American historian has put it in these words: 'The languages of the writers—Greek, Latin, and Spanish—all render the word for soul as a feminine gender noun (psyche, anima, alma). Thus, the extended use of the nuptial metaphor is encouraged by the language (possibly even suggested by it) and not impeded as would be the case in English where the word is neuter, making it awkward to speak of the soul as she.'[11] And there again, it would be interesting to examine whether, on this point as on others, the English translations of the Bible made by Anglicans and Protestants have not been more influenced by the Vulgate than by the original Hebrew.[12]

These biblical and linguistic facts have always played some part in the Christian Western tradition, assuring, as we have already pointed out, the continuity of a certain trend in interpretation. But this does not mean that there was uniformity and rigidity, neither in connection with the Song nor on certain other points—for example, the image that was given of man. Once again, it would seem that we must distinguish, as it were, several middle ages. The first may be characterized as 'patristic', because it prolongs a mode of thought inherited from the Fathers of the Church; this is found more especially in spiritual writings stemming from monastic and canonical milieux, up to the beginning of the thirteenth century. A second middle age may be described as 'scholastic', because of its specific culture developed especially in the town schools, from the beginning of the twelfth century onwards. Lastly, in the course of the same century, there is a secular middle age, that of court literature. To the extent that these different strands of medieval culture coexisted, they influenced each other in a way which, though it is sometimes very subtle and difficult to discern, may not be legitimately ignored.

Thus, in so far as concerns the subject we are dealing with here, it has been possible to pick out some possible if very elusive reminiscences of the Song in a love poem like *Iam, dulcis anima, venito*, written in the tenth century, and also in one of the *Carmina Burana*, a miscellany of liturgical and Goliardic songs of the thirteenth and fourteenth centuries: possibly, we have there 'a slight parody of the sacred epithalamium'. But this 'ironic' use of the Song can only be affirmed for certain in Chaucer, in the fourteenth century and onwards.[13] And yet, in Dante's *Divine Comedy*, which in truth belongs to the class of religious literature, the loving union between the poet and Beatrice is again suggested by means of the biblical imagery relating to Christ and his Bride, the Church: the material and the spiritual, the human and the divine, are, in love, inextricably bound up.[14] We could continue to recall this long and complex history up to the *Spiritual Canticle* of St. John of the Cross, which is obviously inspired by the Song of Songs: the problem of the connections between these two works has now been studied with all possible learning.[15]

As regards the twelfth century, we must get down to a very careful perusal of all the commentaries: these are numerous, the list of them has been drawn up,[16] and their literary and theological tradition has been studied.[17] What now remains to be done is to carry out a vast psychological inquiry on the published works and those which are still unedited, for they do exist. [18] Work on these lines has already been started in connection with St. Bernard.[19] Here, I will give one or two indications as to the method, and then a few examples of monastic commentaries.

III. *A spontaneous symbolism*

Practically the whole Bible is a book of images; but these almost always have, for the medieval Christian, at least two meanings. Whatever may be the precise signification—about which there was never any unanimity—to be given to words such as symbol, allegory, typology, or parable, it is certain that, since, through the history of a given people and in connection with it, the main concern was to narrate the history of universal salvation, any image first conjured up something different from what it actually designated. This ability to interpret everything symbolically was greatly developed in the monastic milieux of the high middle ages, and doubtless also among the clerics, and, though probably to a lesser extent, among the laymen. The difference is explained by the fact that the ability came from an education which not everyone received to the same degree, with the same intensity or continuity.

In the cloister, it was given by a whole complex of living tradition: in the course of the divine office, public and private reading, scriptural texts were constantly heard with the spiritual interpretations which the Fathers and the liturgy had given to the whole Bible, both Old and New Testaments alike. This allegorizing method may have been excessive, perhaps; in particular, it applied to details, to isolated words, a principle of transposition which was only valid for general themes and groups of writings. But it was this method which formed the mentalities of those days. At such a school, it was possible to have, with a minimum of images, of 'things seen', a maximum of symbols, of evoked realities. This result was produced to greater or lesser degrees according to the different personalities, according to whether each one was, so to speak, more or less a 'poet' or a 'reasoner': in the same period we have a man like St. Bernard using more images and symbols than did a man like William of Saint-Thierry, and the same could be said of a man like Peter of Celle compared to Aelred of Rievaulx, just to quote a few examples.

This ability to use symbols and the variety of applications made of them is to be noticed in the interpretation of the Song of Songs as well as in everything else. In the middle ages, more than in our own days, it was not necessary to have personal experience of sexual relations in order to know—and not merely in a very general way—what they implied: the clear allusions made by the Bible sufficed to give the necessary information; some passages even go into details, as in certain pages from the prophets or certain accounts given in the Old Testament.[20] So it was not even necessary to have read Ovid. But other, and many more, scriptural texts gave symbolic meaning to the activity of human love, and used it for evoking God's union with his people and his Church, and with every individual in them. It was normal for the Fathers and the liturgy, whose texts furnished and fashioned the monastic memories, to go even further in the same sense. And let us not forget either that the conditions of life and habitation favouring promiscuity made it possible for young monks to have in their minds the image of fleshly union even before their parents offered them to the monastery: and they sometimes acknowledged quite openly that it 'came to mind',[21] which is only normal and healthy. But on the basis of these images retained from their readings or in their memories, they were able to think of, and take pleasure in, quite different realities, of which the images were symbols.

In the face of this, there is an idea which quite naturally comes to the mind of anyone today who has a smattering of modern psychology, especially if it is of the Freudian type: this idea is that the most important is that about which we do not speak— the unsaid—because it is repressed, but obsessional. Stretching this to extremes, such medieval literature is chaste because its authors were not.

Any such reaction ignores the difference between the 'double meanings' and the 'hidden meanings'. A 'hyper-eroticized society',[22] which has been made such by all sorts of ways— publicity and so forth—and has frequently been exploited for economic and commercial purposes—a consumer society, thus a producer society, favours double meanings; but the hidden meanings are those conveyed by symbols which must be interpreted, and which actually are so by a whole cultural make-up, of which symbolism—including and especially biblical symbolism—is an important part and parcel. This symbolism is in our days being fruitfully studied by psychologists, linguists, and theologians; in the monastic middle ages, it was a natural phenomenon about which no one even thought. Thus, a word and an image can have a double meaning in one culture but not in another.

So we must distinguish between the willed, conscious, intentional double meanings, such as those which are found later on, after the twelfth century and outside monasticism, in Goliardic poetry, or—more artistic and more refined—in authors like Chaucer, and the double meanings which we can describe as being unwitting: modern psychologists suddenly detect them in ancient texts, whereas they were unknown to people in the past. Does this mean that those meanings were just unconscious, or were they conscious and repressed? Even in Christianity today, there are many who use, study, comment on, and sing the Song of Songs without being assailed by the images, associations, and emotional reactions which certain psychologists would suppose—whatever may have been the case with the writer of this biblical poem. Such images, among the majority of readers, belong to the realm of the unknown unconscious. There is one Jew who, since the days when he was first taken to the synagogue as an adolescent, admits that he never thought of anything else when he heard the Song of Songs than God and his people, and it was only when he went to a Western university that any other possible meaning crossed his mind.[23]

Likewise, why should we unjustifiably suspect so many monks and nuns, so many spiritual writers, of being obsessed, repressed men and women, if the texts show that, without any compulsive violence, and with a candid tranquillity which is disarming for us moderns, they gave proof of simplicity rather than duplicity, when they lingered over images which would distract the attention of many of our contemporaries from the divine mystery and turn it towards human behaviour? Are we necessarily obliged to 'scratch' the surface of medieval texts in order to discover, beneath the layers or between the lines, allusions which confirm theories based on a psychology foreign to their culture? Is the argument that silence is telling, that the fact of saying nothing about what some people would spontaneously think of today, proof in favour of taboos, shame, and guilt, or, on the contrary, does it reveal a lack of interest for things which today obsess many people's imagination? For example, when Gilbert of Hoyland

describes the art of emphasizing the beauty of breasts by means
of corsets, he is much more interested in the exigencies of the
laws of rhetoric which he wants to stress in this connection than
with the reality which he took by way of comparison. So, briefly,
we can say that everything points to the fact that, if there were
any double meanings, they worked in the opposite direction than
they do for some people, though not everyone, today. Instead of
going back to repressed images buried in the subconscious, a
double meaning stimulated readers to search for a mysterious
and hidden meaning based on biblical symbols.

How may we now explain that such was the psychological
attitude of monks in the presence of the Song of Songs? By
what processes, method, and education did they come to this
state?

IV. *The school of the liturgy*

The normal way in which monks received the allegorical interpretation of Scripture was, first of all, the liturgy, and this
applies to the Song of Songs as well as to other books, and
perhaps even more so, to the extent that it was 'allegorized'
more than others. The Jewish custom had been, and still is in
many places, to read passages from the Song during the celebration of the Passover and of the Sabbath. In some synagogues
the whole of the Song used to be read—and still is read today—
on each Sabbath, for it recalls God's loving union with his
people. It was only natural that this conception should be handed
down in the liturgy of the Church, and, in fact, the nuptial
symbolism of the Old Testament is to be found in the texts of
the New Testament, and then, by their interpreters in very
early Christian authors, such as Tertullian and Origen, in the
rituals of the Church, and particularly in ceremonies of Christian
initiation: baptism introduces a soul into this great love affair
with God, and in Hippolytus, St. Ambrose, St. Cyril of Alex-
andria, and others, each baptismal rite is symbolically explained
in a more or less artificial way, with allusions to the water, oil,

seal, and other images found in the Song.[24] Thus there existed, in this sense, a very long tradition: no one had to invent the idea that the Song could and should be applied to the Church, to Christian living, nor was it necessary to invent the general meaning which it had in this area.

However, it was during the middle ages that the Song made its solemn entry, so to speak, into that part of the liturgy which left the deepest mark on monastic psychology: the divine office. It first came in from the Marian point of view. From the times of the Fathers, St. Ambrose had suggested that post-exilic themes such as God's fidelity and the mutual love existing between him and his people, evoked by the imagery of the Song and Psalm 44, another nuptial poem, could be applied to the Blessed Virgin.[25] When the feast of the Assumption was accepted in the West, the office that was composed for it, from the middle of the seventh century or during the eighth, contained antiphons which were either taken from the feasts of virgins or else composed especially for the new occasion: several of both kinds had been borrowed from the Song.[26] But there were never any readings from this in the Roman liturgy, though it was used in Milan and Spain.[27] Furthermore, the office lectionary, which we know to have been structured very early on, has, for August, readings from the 'books of Solomon'. This means that the Song was probably read either entirely or in part during the night office. [28] Anything that could not be read or finished in choir was continued in the refectory, reading at table being considered as a continuation of the choir readings. It could also have happened that passages from the Song were read in Chapter, during the daily 'conference'.

This custom, unanimously attested to by canonical collections,[29] was observed in the twelfth century, and especially in Cistercian monasteries.[30] The office of the Assumption also remained unchanged until the great reform of the Cistercian liturgy which took place towards 1147 and in which St. Bernard had some part to play. Among other offices that of the Assumption underwent profound revision, and the most important innovation consisted in the introduction of a series of lyrical antiphons inspired by the Song. In one of the most ancient manuscripts which has been preserved of this renovated liturgy, the modifications made to the text and the melodies were so many that none of the original folios could be kept: one of the revisers had to rewrite it completely.[31] At first Vespers on the eve of the feast, the opening antiphon is taken from a passage of the Song which formerly was placed just before the Magnificat. This first antiphon set the tone for the whole office, and this is maintained throughout until the last antiphon, also drawn from the Song. At the first nocturn of the night office, a complete new series of six antiphons taken from the Song was introduced; these antiphons were also found in the Office for the Nativity of the Virgin. The first of them ran as follows: 'Behold, you are beautiful, my love, behold you are beautiful! Your eyes are doves. . . .' In the office before the reform, three of the four responsories were taken from the Song, and they were retained in the reformed office: but the fourth responsory, which did not come from the Song, was replaced by a new one: 'Daughters of Jerusalem, tell my beloved that I am sick with love. . . .' According to an expert on the matter the melody, which was certainly composed by the Cistercian revisers, has something passionate about it, as do the troubadour songs. The sermon written by a disciple of St. Bernard, Guerric of Igny, for the Assumption, is based on this text. It could well have been preached at Igny at the time when this new responsory was introduced.

In the second nocturn, every one of the antiphons is new, and they are all taken from the Song; they start and end with the word 'Come!' There are more additional extracts from the Song in the third nocturn, and in the long antiphon preceding the Magnificat at second Vespers: 'You are most beautiful, my beloved, . . . come and you shall be crowned!' With this text the feast comes to a close. As for the readings at the night office, on the day of the Assumption, during its octave, and also on the feast of the Nativity of the Virgin, they were all taken from a text by Paschasius Radbert, which was long attributed to St.

Jerome, and in which there is abundant imagery from the Song.

These details concerning liturgical history are of noteworthy importance, for they authorize certain conclusions. Firstly, they prove that the allegorical use of the Song in the course of community prayer derives from a very long-standing tradition. Then they show that this poem was quite naturally interpreted and closely connected with virginity, the virginity of Mary and that of all holy virgins. When people wanted to talk about other realities, they looked to other sources. But the nuptial symbolism was always evoked for virginity, either in liturgical texts drawn directly from the Song of Songs, or in other texts such as the one we have for the feast of Mary's Purification: 'Sion, adorn your bridal chamber. . . .'[32] Moreover it is easy to understand that when the Cistercians reformed their liturgy in 1147, they made extensive use of extracts from the Song, upon which St. Bernard had been working for twelve years. The successive series of sermons which he had already composed on this poem were circulating in the Order and in the whole Church, and they had met with success which explains the revived interest for this book of the Bible.[33] Finally, the fact that St. Bernard gave no Marian interpretation to the Song is significant; it proves that any such interpretation was transmitted by the liturgy, and Bernard himself furthered its importance even more in the new offices. But being a creative man, Bernard remains free with regard to any model, and in his great work on the Song he extends the application of the symbolism it contains to the whole Church and to each of its members.

v. *A methodical formation*

This education in symbolism was given not only by a monastic background, but was also inculcated by a real methodology. This was mainly applied to profane texts, it is true, but it could not fail to affect other spheres as well. This method consisted in reading the *accessus*, that is to say those 'introductions' to 'authors' which taught readers to interpret everything in an ethical sense. By way of example, let us examine a work of this kind written by Conrad of Hirsau in his mature years, towards 1124 or 1125, at the very time when St. Bernard was only just starting to write. When Conrad comes to Aesop's fables, it might be thought that since these were already moralizing tales, there was no need for transposition. Yet all the considerations which he exposes or supposes about man are immediately interpreted by Conrad at a religious level. And he even almost equates Aesop with the sacred authors, and in this sense raises him to their rank, since they also borrowed comparisons from the animal world in order to teach morals. His intention, so it would appear, was to teach men to master their animal instincts.[34] We are free, if we so wish, to find that the note is forced or artificial; but, for Conrad and his pupils, and others of their kind, it went without saying that every one of God's creatures has a message to give in view of his kingdom and of the ways which lead there. Thus they unhesitatingly gave posthumous baptism, so to say, to these profane authors.

But this did not happen in an automatic way. It met with resistance, and effort had to be put forth to overcome this. Justifications were called for, and objections had to be answered, such as those which Conrad in his *Dialogue* puts into the mouth of the disciple, who asks, 'Does not divine knowledge make these texts useless?'[35] And the master replies that the problem is not as easy as all that in this connection, and goes on to acknowledge the ambiguity of these pagan writers, since there is good and bad in their writings. So they have to be despised and yet esteemed, or, more precisely, allegorized, that is to say given a meaning which they did not fully realize themselves. Horace, for example, does expose his reader to some moral danger when he describes the vices.[36] And this again is a remark made by the pupil: and it is not at all by chance that it should be he who sees the difficulty. However, the master, who is already formed, can be more optimistic. 'Yes,' he says, 'but one has to be indulgent towards such men who, according to St. Paul, could well have had natural knowledge of God, but they were not helped by revelation. It is this which explains that we find in them matter for admiration and matter for excuse.'[37]

Throughout Conrad's *Dialogue on the Authors* it would be possible to pick out similar invitations to allegorize profane texts in the same way that was done for sacred texts. The aim in both cases is identical: the profit to be drawn from reading: 'The final cause for reading is the fruit. . . .'[38] 'The milk with which the poets nurture you must become the source of more solid food, that is to say, of loftier reading. . . .'[39] 'In the writings of a man of secular learning we must always seek out some higher wisdom',[40] even though we may have to eliminate anything which would be contrary to this.[41] A little further on, poetry or *Poetria*, that is to say the set of laws binding upon the poet, is compared to a lovely woman whose beauty lends perfection to words and ideas.[42] Not only must we make use of all that is good in pagan authors, as did St. Paul, St. Jerome, St. Augustine, and so many others;[43] but we must even go so far as to be clever enough to find this out and to distinguish it from what is less good or even frankly bad: thus, in certain of Ovid's works, we find gold which stinks of the muck in which it is buried.[44] But wherever it is possible to interpret a text or fact favourably, for the purpose of being edified, that is to say, of getting some fruit out of reading, then it must be done, and this is something that can be learnt. This is why Bernard of Utrecht, towards the end of the eleventh century, declares, at the end of his preface to the *Commentary of Theodulus*, a tenth-century Latin poet: 'I have explained the *Eclogue* of Theodulus, first according to the literal meaning, then according to the allegorical meaning, and also, in many places, in a moral sense.'[45]

These interpretative texts, which are merely a few witnesses among many others, give us a glimpse of the spiritual and psychological problem facing medieval monks. There was an antinomy only partly resolved between the profane and the sacred texts. The result was, on the one hand, an attitude of suspicion, even of guilt, towards profane literature,[46] and, on the other hand, the conviction that this patrimony of human culture ought not to be lost because it had some real value. Hence the necessity of attempting to reconcile the two. Now the psychological mechanism implied in all the literary forms of the period made this synthesis quite possible, on condition of using what would seem to us to be a subterfuge. This consisted in using a filter, as it were, on the authors, and thus sifting out the persons and things they wrote about; thereby discerning a certain evil which called for prudence, as well as some acceptable good. It was as if the evil were exorcized from the pagan author—and unconsciously from his reader as well—and attributed to his ignorance of God, or else to the tempter, the devil. And one only mirrored oneself in those passages which were in keeping with Christian morals, these being considered as the most authentic message of the profane writer, the better part in him, unconsciously influenced by God. This was the author's true self, worthy of admiration.

Thus by relating images and facts to God, people were able to sanctify them to the utmost. Conrad of Hirsau, and others like him, are very sure of themselves in the statements they make. But occasionally, Conrad's embarrassed explanations, and especially the hesitations which he puts into the mouth of his disciple—thus giving to understand that he himself had none—suggest that the basic project was not so much a matter of finding a key to interpreting ancient texts with an aim to scientific study as that of solving a personal problem. We cannot help thinking that there had been some kind of struggle going on in him about these profane authors, who, though they were admirable in themselves, were dangerous, and this he had fought so as to gain the upper hand. We could hardly dare say that he and others had always been successful. This alternation between admiration and distrust continues to be evident in many spiritual writers. The presence in them of problems which had been surmounted, but not entirely eliminated, and which even occasionally surfaced in their consciences, makes them very human, very close to Christians of all times, even though in later centuries the way in which the problems are formulated may vary.

VI. *From images to realities*

In the Bible the question is not always solely one of God's
relationship with his people and with the whole of mankind.
Instead we often find mentioned realities which are part of any
human relationship: for instance the love relationship, which is
often simply a symbol of the former kind. Thus we find in Holy
Scripture a whole language dealing with *eros*, whose function, as
may be divined, is to evoke *agape*, charity. We may query
whether the passage from one level to the other was always easy
for spiritual medieval authors. Was it helped by the education
received from the monastic background, so deeply stamped by
the Fathers and the liturgy and by the allegorizing techniques
applied to profane authors?

Before examining examples taken from commentaries on the
Song of Songs, let us first go through two short texts in which the
vocabulary of sexuality, borrowed from the Bible, is used with a
fair degree of precision. Let us start with the long *Lament on
abandoned quiet and solitude*, in which John of Fécamp, from the
outset, converses with the tranquillity of the solitary life as with
some 'chaste' companion:[47] 'Who snatched you away from me?
Formerly I gave myself up entirely to your embracing arms, and
I clung with joy, with all my mind, to your most pure kiss. Who
snatched me away from your embraces, O my loved lady?' This
ardent dialogue, a sort of letter of love, and separated love at
that, is full of reminiscences of the Song of Songs, of Virgil's
Bucolics and *Georgics*, and it abounds in poetic images taken from
the Bible, St. Jerome, St. Gregory, Ovid, Martial, Juvenal, and
other classical authors. The entire vocabulary is one of human
love, even though it deals with union with God. And suddenly,
in order to evoke his rape from solitude, John of Fécamp recalls
the violence which Dinah, Jacob's daughter, suffered in the past,
and which is narrated in detail in the Book of Genesis.[48] There
was no necessity to relate this incident: an allusion would have
been enough. But when John of Fécamp does so he gives it a
wealth of psychological nuances; whereas he is content with

briefly summarizing the dramatic ending, he spends some time in suggesting that this sentimental episode is quite possibly true. He obviously enjoys writing this piece of literature: he chooses his words carefully, and the use of diminutives betrays the pre-occupations of an author. John of Fécamp depicts Dinah as imprudently venturing out, alone and without permission, satis-fying her curiosity, showing off her beauty, letting herself be seduced, and losing all self-control, until her honour was avenged by her brothers.[49] Now why should there be any pleasure in such reading if not because, as John of Fécamp says, it has a 'typical meaning'?[50] Is it an example of what befalls any sinner, even though his unfaithfulness consisted in nothing more than letting himself be carried away under the stress of circumstances and with the best of intentions, from a solely contemplative life? Could there be any stronger contrast between the level of the real event, what happened to Dinah, and the highly spiritual conflict which went on in John of Fécamp, a hermit by desire, who had yet become a reformer and abbot in spite of himself?

This same facility for passing from the language of one order of experience to quite another appears in a text which dates from shortly after: St. Anselm's *Meditation* entitled *Lamentation on lost Virginity*. The definitive title says, 'unhappily lost or in sore straits', whereas it is described as being 'lost by fornication'[51] in the first draft.[52] Anselm starts out by communing with his own soul, then with sinning man in general, that is to say, all mankind. In forceful formulas, by means of vehement castigations, he speaks of adultery, unfaithfulness with regard to Christ. Since it is the soul who is in question, the whole discourse is in the feminine. She has been unfaithful, not so much because she has given way to solicitations coming from the flesh, nor because she has been accomplice to an *affaire* between a man and a woman, but because she has let herself be seduced away from God to the Demon, away from the state of grace to sin. The crude language of adultery is thus transposed, all through an introduction, to what is in reality a meditation on God's judgement of man, on hell which he has merited, and on the mercy which will be shown him. The fundamental conviction can be summed up in an avowal which every Christian can make his own: 'I am a sinner, Lord, I am a sinner.' At the end of this meditation on judgement, the theme of lost virginity gives opportunity for a conclusion in the same strains as the introduction.

The idea that is always taken for granted is that the soul is the bride of Christ: as long as she does not sin, she is a virgin, but if she does commit sin, then she loses her virginity. Now, every man is a sinner, and so the forceful images taken from the language of impurity are applicable to him, and they are re-enforced by contrasting plays on words: 'O virginity, you who were once my loved one, and whom I have lost . . .![53] O fornication, it was you who caused my loss. . . . O my soul . . . adulterous, unfaithful to Christ, wretched creature that you are, of your own free will you plunged down from the sublime heights of virginity into the abyss of fornication. Was it not you who were once wedded to the King of heaven? Brazenly, you have now given yourself in prostitution to hell's executioner . . . and you have embraced the devil. . . .[54] You obstinate prostitute, you impudent fornicatress, God was your lover, and of yourself, you proposed divorce, you ran headlong, instinctively, towards the man who had set a trap for you, and so you lost yourself. . . . You united with the evil one, with foolish impurity and filthy iniquity. What have you done? You have abandoned your chaste heavenly lover in order to follow into hell your hateful corrupter. In this abyss it is not a marriage-bed that he has prepared for you, but a paramour's couch. . . .'[55]

Modern sensitivity would probably have brought this sort of comparison to an end earlier on, for the reading of it, especially in translation, embarrasses us. But a man like Anselm of Canterbury, a very refined, delicate, spiritual writer and a subtle dialectician, a man who was a compassionate abbot, a daring archbishop, finds pleasure in it, and he comes back to it before concluding his eulogy on the mercy of the Lord: 'If virginity, once it is deflowered, cannot, Oh unhappy thing, recover her reward, at least she can, by repenting, avoid the pain due to

fornication. . . .'[56] The aim of this text was to rouse up a feeling
of guilt, and then to transform it into an occasion for hope. And
this aim was attained, because there was no unhealthy, depressing
lingering over the responsibility of the fault. On the contrary,
the whole development and even its last words, are related to
pardon. But in order to pave the way for this, a sexual symbolism
inspired by the Bible offered vocabulary and style which, because
they were in Latin, were probably less crude. It is possible that
the imaginative charge of these words and allusions was reduced,
in comparison with the intense evocation of the joys of regained
union with God. Scripture had enough texts on love and on
adultery for the reader to be acquainted with these realities. But
it also had other and even more texts which allowed him to
interpret these on the interior level, and the universal level of the
relations between man and God.

VII. *Different keys to interpretation*

Within the same symbolism, there was room for different interpretations, according to the applications of nuptial images to the
various aspects of the mystery of salvation and its accomplishment in the course of human history. There are numerous texts
to illustrate this remark.

First, we have an example of an ecclesiological interpretation,
with strong political overtones, of the Song of Songs.[57] This was
written by John of Mantua, an author about whom we know
nothing for certain, but who drafted, probably between 1081
and 1083, a commentary at the request of Countess Matilda, to
whom other authors had also dedicated spiritual writings.[58] She
was a patron of the Roman Church, and fulfilled her duty by
helping Gregory VII and taking up his defence against his
enemies, the emperor Henry IV and the bishops who made up
his party—especially those in Lombardy. The only originality
about this commentary lies in the clear allusions which its author
makes to the events of the times. It conforms to the tradition
issuing from Origen in showing, from the start, that the text of

the Song is a source of teaching for Christian living, because it insists on the fact that it transmits a doctrine of contemplation.[59] It is a 'theoretical', that is to say a contemplative, discourse, as St. Bernard says. John of Mantua is also in the line of the liturgical tradition when he presents Mary as being the model of contemplation at its highest when she was assumed into heaven.[60] But he is not satisfied with merely universal considerations which are applicable to all Christians. He is also composing a work specifically adapted to the person it is intended to encourage.

Now, Matilda is 'persecuted' by Henry IV because of her close alliance with Gregory VII,[61] who, a few years earlier—in 1077 or 1078—had brought Berengar of Tours back to the common faith of the Church about the eucharist. This leads John of Mantua to give precise developments about the real presence. More recently, in 1080 or 1082, the Pope had excommunicated Henry IV, who had thus become heretical and schismatic. Consequently our commentator makes practical applications of the text of the Song to the life of a person, Matilda: she is 'a true bride of God', she who out of love, like the bride in the Song, has gone about all the streets of the city in order to find her beloved: she never ceases searching for him, and her 'love arises' from her contemplation.[62] But this must be reconciled with her 'active life', a formula which is frequently used here when speaking of her political activity. The countess must oppose by every means within her power—including that of armed force—both the excommunicated emperor, and his bishops, and all who by their allegiance to him have become heretics. She must take up the cause of the only true 'King of the Romans', the Pope. Thus, says John of Mantua in conclusion, she will be like the bride in the Song, a model of both contemplation and activity, that is to say of 'labour' in God's service.[63]

Such political allusions do not occur on every page. But they are frequent enough and sufficiently precise and insistent for us to be able to grasp that politics is the underlying preoccupation of the whole commentary. Thus, we have here an 'epithalamium',

that is to say, a nuptial song about marriage-bed activities—
thalamus[64]—being used as a pretext for exhorting to immediate
action. There is never a question of anything but love, which can
be shown in several ways, one of which is the Christian wielding
of power. Whenever we wish to speak of love, in whatever field,
we are obliged to use the language of love, and this is possible
since it can be interpreted in different ways: Solomon wanted 'to
compose the Song with a number of meanings'.[65]

The Marian interpretation of the Song was sometimes clothed
in a didactic form, for the biblical text offers occasion for stating
truths about the Virgin and her role in the work of salvation: she
was the mother of our Saviour, associated with his life and
passion and the paschal experiences of the nascent Church.
However, even when speaking of Mary, it was possible to use
the Song in different ways. The most widespread was that found
in the liturgy, and in particular for the feast of the Assumption.
The office begins with a question phrased in terms of the Song:
'Who is this coming up like the dawn at daybreak?' The answer
is given at Matins in formulas from the Song inaugurating a
dialogue similar to many others which make many liturgical
dramas so alive: 'Behold! You are beautiful, my love . . .'. Eyes,
lips, perfumes, and charms are all evoked. Let the loved one come
and union be consummated! Such intimate, intense union was
fulfilled to the highest point among human creatures in Mary at
the moment of the Incarnation. But it was only fully accomplished when the Mother of God was taken up into paradise.
Meanwhile it was, for her also, a time of desire: 'O that he would
kiss me, for I am sick with love!' All nature, the flowers and
sweet-smelling spices are associated with this ever-growing joy.
Such contemplative poetry is content with repeating the praises
of the loved one. Everything is centred on her here, and especially
on her fidelity. For her love had been put to the test by a long
separation.

In Mary is renewed the whole drama played throughout the
Song. In the liturgy the antiphons generally follow the order of
the verses in the biblical poem, and so there was no need for any

commentary. The mere expression of this reciprocal search sufficed to suggest not only Mary's love for the Word, her bridegroom now become her child, but also the love of God's son for
her. In the antiphons drawn from the Song, Mary is not named,
but it is always she who is concerned. It is understandable that
when music was needed for the new texts, quite naturally it was
troubadour airs which were composed. This is truly a love poem,
a sort of short romance in which the adventure is not actually
described but simply suggested, discreetly evoked. In the last
antiphon, a miscellany of images picked out here and there in the
Song resumes all the preceding themes, as in some well-
composed symphony. Thus we have admiration, desire, and
possession: 'Winter is past, the rain is over and gone . . . Arise,
my love, my fair one, come from Lebanon, and you shall be
crowned . . .' In this way there is a constant, easy, and effortless
transposition, which, by virtue of its facility, is apt for expressing
a contemplative attitude, joyful consent to the greatness of the
mystery being celebrated. This is pure poetry, not only in the
sense that it is chaste, but also in that it is not intended to
enunciate ideas but to be quite simply poetry, and nothing else:
it is as disinterested and gratuitous as a dialogue between lovers.

Lastly, the most beautiful and the most rightly renowned commentary on the Song is that written by St. Bernard. It is very
revealing of his own psychology, his reactions to the 'feminine',
his monastic and ecclesial preoccupations, and especially his
theology. Even before these sermons, he had already introduced
and commented on verses of the Song in his first writings on love,
his Letter 11 and the treatise *On the Necessity of Loving God*. But
his commentary on the Song is the most prolix of the works
which he devotes to Solomon's poem. Even though, in the series
of eighty-six sermons, he explains only the first two chapters of
the biblical text and the first verse of chapter three, they contain
a complete Christology, for Bernard illustrates there the mystery
and effects of the redemptive Incarnation. He shows how divine
life penetrates the Church as a whole and each particular mem-
ber. Two levels of thought are always to be discerned in this

writing: the relationship of Christ with his Church, and the relationship of the Word with the soul, who, by sanctification, personalizes and thus fulfills all that is universal and objective in the economy of salvation.

Now, this doctrine is proposed in connection with images found in the love song. From the start there is a close parallelism established between the facts mentioned by the Song and those accomplished in Christ. The very title of the poem, says St. Bernard, signifies 'the greatest among the songs', and we are setting out to consider the greatest of all events. The name Solomon means Peacemaker, and Jesus brought us peace symbolized by the kiss: in the Incarnation lay our reconciliation. Once Bernard has stated these facts, he comes round to describing the process by which they came about: the kiss of the mouth is the union of the divinity with our humanity, the communication of the Holy Spirit in mutual love. The breasts which are more lovely than wine signify the fruitfulness of incarnated love shown forth by the patience and steadfast love of Jesus. And so he goes on. Then follow the results of the mystery: 'The upright rightly love you.' Uprightness is the image of God restored in man once bowed down, bent towards earth by sin. The swarthy beauty of the bride is nothing other than the divinity really present in Christ but hidden under the appearances of his humanity: it is grace truly bestowed yet not totally manifested. The other effects of the Incarnation are also exposed and then are applied to the entire Church, to those communities of religious who strive to live this mystery to the utmost: they are, for the bride and the bridegroom, a flower-bedecked couch. Sleep represents contemplation; the ecstasy of love suggests that most elevated state of prayer which takes the soul out of herself. The rising up is the moment when the soul goes forth to undertake 'labour' in the Lord's vineyard. This culminates in eschatology: 'Arise, my love, my fair one and come away, let me hear your voice.' The Church is awaiting and desiring lasting rest. Daybreak, the end of darkness, comes when faith is transformed into vision. The return of the beloved, leaping like a gazelle over the mountains and hills, is the second coming of he who shall come to judge the living and the dead.

All this doctrine is padded with biblical quotations, embellished with comparisons evoking or describing human situations. It is not difficult to see why this mingling of poetry and dogmatics should have at once nurtured and charmed so many minds. The biographer of a thirteenth-century mystic from Liège, Julian of Mount Cornillon, she who requested and obtained the institution of the feast of Corpus Christi, writes a very significant passage worthy of our attention here: 'Since the writings of Blessed Bernard seemed to her so full of mighty flame and sweeter than honey and the honeycomb, she read and embraced them with very much devotion, honouring this saint with the privilege of an immense love. Her whole mind was absorbed with his teaching: she took pains to learn by heart, and fix in her memory once and for all, more than twenty of the sermons in the last part of his commentary on the Song, there where he seems to have outstripped all human knowledge.' Why did Julian read and learn this bridal song of Christ and his Church, of the Word and the soul? 'She was ardently enamoured of these love songs because the language of love was a familiar tongue for her, not a foreign language, for she herself was in love. Indeed, since the days of maidenhood, she had vowed all her love to Christ, she who as a virgin gave herself up to the virginal Christ, the Son of the Virgin. Happy virgin, espoused to Christ before she could be sullied by the world's embrace. And the more maturely she was united with him, so the more blissfully too. When Julian talked to her sisters, she spoke of God, and her discourse came from the abundance of her heart.' It is suggested, then, that she transmitted what she had received from St. Bernard's *Sermons on the Song*. And further on mention is made of an ailment which her sisters attributed to physical infirmity, whereas in actual fact it was the 'sickness of love' spoken of by the bride in the Canticle.[66] Interest in this love poem was not the monopoly of monks and nuns. A feudal lord such as Baudouin of Guines was also taken up with it: 'He had the Song of Songs translated from Latin into the romance tongue and it was read to him frequently, not only in its literal sense, but also according to the spiritual interpretation. This was in view of the mystical interpretation of these Songs.'[67] We know that other translations of the Song of Songs were made at the end of the twelfth century and the beginning of the thirteenth. They were held in suspicion, not because they made this particular text—and other biblical and patristic books—available in the vernacular, but because of the clandestine use made of them by certain sects. A manuscript from Le Mans has preserved a text which is not a translation but a paraphrase of the Song; it has been written in Picard dialect for a lady and other lay people of a small court in Northern France, who were interested in the spiritual interpretation of the biblical love poem, not in an erotic reading of it. In this paraphrase are to be found some themes which come from Origen and had been transmitted, it seems, through St. Bernard and through Geoffrey of Auxerre.[68]

Many other witnesses wrote in the same strain, and an extraordinarily abundant manuscript tradition throughout Europe testifies to the success which this masterpiece enjoyed everywhere.[69] In it there was matter for the enlightenment of faith, as well as the conversion, stimulation, and elevation of the imagination, for it proposed an object worthy of both the redeemed soul and God. In the period with which we are dealing, and in this particular region of Champagne, all through the years of medieval Christianity, where, in castles and courts, in townships and among the people, love literature was so largely cultivated, it was Bernard, among all the lyric writers, who was the most popular and by far the most widely read. It was not in his letters to women —noble ladies or nuns—that he gave free vent to the love which burned in his heart, but it was to his monks, when he spoke about the love which had united Solomon to his beloved, and which continued to unite the true Solomon to his Church. Each one recognized in what Bernard said the expression of his own faith and his own aspirations. This is always something more than the bare sense intimated by the text of the Song, but that something is linked with the images it proposes. Bernard taught by images as from a springboard, and soared above them by a constant and natural allegorizing process. Monastic society, where there is more reading, song, and love than in secular society, also needed its trouvère: St. Bernard was this God-given man.

VIII. *In the lineage of St. Bernard*

Since we cannot possibly peruse every commentary on the Song of Songs subsequent to St. Bernard, let us restrict ourselves to the one written by Geoffrey of Auxerre, a former pupil of Abelard become disciple of the abbot of Clairvaux. This commentary has been preferred to others because it is as yet unstudied, having been edited only recently. It is also one of the longest and rarest complete commentaries, explaining the whole of the text. Doubtless it is less original than others, in the sense that it is partly a compilation of extracts from previous commentaries, especially those by Bernard, Bede, and Gilbert of Hoyland. Yet it does have many passages which are specific to it, and even with those which are not, the fact that the author selected one or other passage or interpretation is revealing of his intentions.

From the beginning, the images of the Song are related to similar terms in the New Testament. The 'cellars' in which are kept the reserves and treasures lead one to think of 'the hidden treasures of wisdom and knowledge' mentioned by the epistle to the Colossians.[70] Likewise, anything connected with human love immediately recalls purely spiritual biblical symbolisms.[71] There is never anything erotic, not even a fleeting hint. The strongest images become the most innocent: 'While the king was on his couch . . .' is transposed, for the couch is the bosom of the Father.[72] The bag of myrrh is the community of monks resting between the two breasts in order to be nourished alternately to the right and to the left with spiritual and bodily food.[73] Between the breasts, it is remarked, and not upon the shoulders, for it is not a burden; but upon the breast, like someone dearly loved,

and with love everything becomes lightsome.[74] Whole pages are
devoted to the interpretations concerning the bed, which is 'the
tranquillity of the cenobites',[75] 'each person's conscience',[76] 'the
repose of holy contemplation',[77] and so forth. Not once does
Geoffrey seem to remember that a bed is first of all a bed. 'Behold
you are beautiful, my love.'[78] Throughout this praise of the bride
there is nothing but symbols, there is not a single visual image.
The two breasts, when they are admired, 'mean the teaching
about faith and morals'.[79] The 'belly' is the conscience, or the
weakness which obliges us to acknowledge that we are unfit for
such or such office.[80] 'I had put off my garment . . . they took away
my mantle . . .' can only mean that we are to renounce the old
man in us in order to put on the new man.[81] Explanations of this
sort follow on through about fifteen pages. 'I held him and would
not let him go . . .': this citation introduces all those passages
in the Bible where the verb 'to hold' is found, and they flow from
the commentator's pen: 'Old Simeon held the child Jesus and
did not let him go . . . and the psalmist says, "You have held me
by the right hand, and led me according to your will".'[82] Sometimes Geoffrey reproduces a passage which sketches a description like the one of the bride's cheeks: 'I cannot help being gently
moved when I depict for myself such a face . . .', but he quickly
turns aside and thinks of other cheeks than those of a maiden.[83]
And it is the same for the charm added to the breasts by their
swelling.[84] And the legs of the bridegroom do not interest him
either.[85]

We have now come to the description of the bride contained in
the last two chapters and to which 150 pages are devoted. At the
start of this section a dedicatory letter announces that we shall be
dealing 'in the first place with the universal Church, secondly
with the monastic community, and thirdly the spiritual soul'.[86]
And in fact all we have is ideas, hardly any images, or even none
at all. Geoffrey several times comments upon the 'belly' and the
'navel' without lingering over them, almost as though they did
not ever come before his mind's eye. Since it is in the 'belly' that
conception takes place, it is the symbol of a community of

cloistered monks which forms within itself new members.[87] As for the 'navel', since it is a hollow, a 'crater', and so a sort of reservoir, it represents 'joyful devotion'[88] and the 'wealth of consolation'.[89] 'The joints of your legs are like well-turned jewels'. Geoffrey's attention is retained not by the legs themselves, but by the fact that the Latin word used is *iunctura*—which leads us to think of all that unites, thus of peace, concord, reconciliation, a good understanding, communion, charity, so many spiritual realities about which he is an inexhaustible source.[90] Now this is a formula which could well have aroused in another mind quite different images.

Finally, many pages explain the invitation addressed to the young man by the fiancée, to follow her into her mother's house,[91] with the reminder of what happened to this latter underneath the apple tree.[92] What could easily have become the most realistic description is the one which is least imagined, and even the least 'seen'. Nothing is eroticized, and whatever there is of the erotic in the Song ceases to be so under the author's pen.

Geoffrey of Auxerre worked for many long years over this vast commentary, several parts of which are dedicated to various different people who had asked him to write it and especially to bring it to completion. He was acknowledged to be competent in this field. From this point of view he can be considered as an average witness, a normal witness, as it were, of monastic exegesis of the Song of Songs in the twelfth century.[93] There are still other and better commentaries on the Song dating from the same period, and each has its particular characteristics determined by the preoccupations of the man who wrote it: William of Saint-Thierry gives more room to theology, and Gilbert of Hoyland to psychology. Of them all, St. Bernard is the man who best succeeds in allying a very human accent to an immense wealth of poetic images, ideas, allusions to men and events of his times. It is with him that the allegorical process is the least artificial. But there is one essential point on which his commentary on the Song greatly resembles the one written by Geoffrey of Auxerre, whom he first converted and then formed. This is something which might well seem in our times hardly credible, but even so it is a fact that more than 600 pages of representative texts allow us to observe,[94] on the basis of the strongest possible evidence—that the monastic commentaries on the Song of Songs are witnesses not only to a chaste literature, but also to an equally chaste milieu, an equally chaste love.

[1] Ecclus. 42: 12-14. Another even longer development of the same kind is found in ibid. 25: 17-36. M. Morreale has studied a thirteenth-century Castilian translation of this text: 'Latin y castellano en un romanceamento biblico del S. XIII: Lectura de Eccl. 25, 24-28', 'Homenaje a Artura Marasso', *Cuadernos del Sur*, 11 (1975), pp. 19-24.

[2] E. Faral, *Dictionnaire des lettres françaises*, published under the direction of G. Grente, *Le moyen âge*, Paris, 1966, 'Introduction', p. 12.

[3] 'Docet de solo amore Dei', *Biblia sacra cum glossis, Praefatio in librum Canticum canticorum*, III, Antwerp, 1634, 1826. Equally revealing is the beginning of a sermon contained in the manuscript, Paris, B.N. lat. 1595, fo. 196: *Vulnerata caritate . . . Istud verbum scribitur in Canticis id est in libro de amoribus spiritualibus . . .*

[4] There is not much to retain from the rapid historical synthesis in which more than twenty centuries of literary history are summarized and interpreted by William E. Phipps, in his own way: 'The Plight of the Song of Songs', *Journal of the Academy of Religion*, 42 (1974), pp. 82-100. On this article, cf. 'Agressivité et répression chez Bernard de Clairvaux', *Revue d'histoire de la spiritualité*, 52 (1976), pp. 155-72.

[5] Art. 'Cantique des Cantiques', in *Dictionnaire de spiritualité*, II (1953), cols. 86-109. A. Robert, R. Tournay, and A. Feuillet, *Le Cantique des cantiques. Traduction et commentaire*, Paris, 1963, pp. 43-55.

[6] L. Krinetzki, 'Die erotische Psychologie des Hohen Liedes', *Theologische Quartalschrift*, 150 (1970), pp. 404-16.

[7] See below, Ch. VI, second paragraph.

[8] H. J. Mathews, 'Anonymous Commentary on the Song of Songs. Edited from a unique manuscript in the Bodleian Library', in *Festschrift . . . zum 80en Geburtstag Moritz Steinschneider*, 1896, p. 239.

[9] Ibid., p. 240. The exceptional nature of the text is confirmed by the fact that it is found in a single, late manuscript: ibid., p. 238.

[10] Ch. A. Bernard, 'La fonction symbolique en spiritualité', *Nouvelle revue théologique*, 95 (1973), pp. 1130-1.

[11] R. Whitson, *Mysticism and Ecumenism*, New York, 1966, p. 46.

[12] R. S. H. Boyd, *India and the Latin Captivity of the Church. The Cultural Context of the Gospel*, Cambridge, 1974, pp. 61-3: 'The Influence of the Vulgate'. Let us note in passing that the allegorical interpretation of the Song has been kept up in the Protestant tradition, as has been established by G. L. Scheper, 'Reformation Attitudes toward Allegory and the Song of Songs', *PMLA* 89 (1974), pp. 551-62.

[13] On all this, cf. J. I. Wimsatt, 'Chaucer and the Canticle of Canticles', in *Chaucer the Love Poet*, ed. Jerome Mitchell and William Provost, University of Georgia Press, Athens, 1973, pp. 66-90; the same texts, and others are also cited by P. Dronke, *Medieval Latin and the Rise of European Love-Lyric*, Oxford, 1968, vol. II, pp. 484 and 515 (whereas the passage quoted from the Song, ibid., p. 338, could have provided very much more precise allusions); by Roy J. Pearcy, 'Modes of Signification and the Humor of Obscene Diction in the Fabliaux', in *The Humor of the Fabliaux*, ed. T. D. Cooke and R. L. Honeycutt, University of Missouri Press, 1974, p. 176; by E. Kohler, *Sociologia del*

Fin'amor. Saggi trobadorici, Padua, 1976, pp. 206 and 230; and by others. During a conference held at Louvain in May 1977 on the Bible in the Middle Ages, P. Dronke presented a very erudite commentary on the poem *Iam dulcis amica venito*; from the text, with apparatus, which he distributed, it appears that there are only four reminiscences of the Song, whereas there are five of Ovid and a total of thirteen reminiscences of classical poets. Furthermore, the author of the poem borrows few stylistic ornaments from the Song, whereas the authors of the many and long monastic commentaries on the Song develop broader and deeper themes, such as the dialectic of presence and absence, the meaning of search and desire, and so forth.

¹⁴ See below, the Epilogue.

¹⁵ F. Pépin, *Noces de feu. Le Symbolisme nuptial du 'Cantico espiritual' de S. Jean de la Croix à la lumière du Canticum Canticorum*, Paris–Tournai–Montreal, 1972, p. 434; in particular, on the problem evoked in the preceding note, Ch. I, pp. 23–75: 'Le symbolisme nuptial: le thème et sa problématique'.

¹⁶ A. Cabassut and M. Olphe-Gailliard, art., 'Cantique des Cantiques: Au moyen âge', in *Dictionnaire de spiritualité*, II, Paris, 1953, cols. 101–4.

¹⁷ F. Ohly, *Hohelied-Studien. Gründzüge einer Geschichte der Hoheleidauslegung des Abendländes bis um 1200*, Wiesbaden, 1958; H. Riedlinger, *Die Makellosigkeit der Kirche in den lateinischen Hoheliedkommentaren des Mittelalters*, Münster, 1958. The bibliography on the subject is increasing constantly. A good over-all view has been given by Emero S. Stegman Jr., *The Language of Asceticism in St. Bernard of Clairvaux's 'Sermones super Cantica canticorum'*, New York, 1973 (University Microfilms, Ann Arbor, Michigan), pp. 56–9.

¹⁸ For example, that of Gilbert of Stanford, presented in *Analecta Monastica*, I, Rome (*Studia Anselmiana*, 20), 1948, pp. 205–30 (with indication of unedited texts, pp. 206–7); the one which may be attributed to Helinand of Froidmont or to Odo of Cheriton, presented in *Archives d'hist. doctr. et litt. du moyen âge*, 31 (1964), pp. 37–59; 32 (1965), pp. 61–9. And still others.

¹⁹ 'S. Bernard et le féminin', in *Nouveau visage de Bernard de Clairvaux. Approches psycho-historiques*, Paris, 1976, pp. 127–54; E. S. Stegman Jr., op. cit.

²⁰ For example, in Hosea, *passim*; in Ezekiel 16; the story of Tamar, in 2 Samuel 13; of the daughters of Moab, in Numbers 25, etc.

²¹ E. Mikkers, 'Un "Speculum novitii" inédit d'Etienne de Salley', in *Collectanea Ord. Cist. Ref.* 8 (1946), p. 45. 15–18.

²² The expression is from J. M. Domenach, 'Libération ou le nouvel ordre sexuel', *Esprit*, 43 (1975), p. 92.

²³ This witness has often been given in public by A. Chouraqui, who alludes to it in the introduction to his excellent translation of the Song entitled: 'Le poème des poèmes', in *La Bible. Les cinq volumes*, Paris, 1975, p. 27.

²⁴ J. Daniélou, *Bible et liturgie*, Paris, 1951, pp. 259–80.

²⁵ A. Robert, 'La Sainte Vierge dans l'Ancien Testament', in *Maria. Études sur la Sainte Vierge*, I, Paris, 1949, pp. 31–3.

²⁶ Dom Capelle, 'La liturgie mariale en Occident', ibid., p. 225, with bibliography; G. Frénaud, 'Marie et l'Église d'après les liturgies du VIIᵉ au XIᵉ siècle', *Études mariales*, 9 (1951), pp. 54–5; C. Barré, 'Antiennes et répons de la Vierge', *Marianum*, 29 (1967), pp. 226–30.

²⁷ For Milan, G. Godu, art. 'Épîtres', in *Diction. d'archéol. chrét. et de lit.* V. 1, Paris, 1922, cols. 296–7; For Spain: J. Perez de Urbel, *Liber commicus*, II, p. 459.

²⁸ This is evidenced by the various *Ordines romani* (XIII A, n. 8, XIV, etc.), for example, ed. M. Andrieu, *Les Ordines romani du haut moyen âge*, II, Louvain, 1948, p. 484, etc.

²⁹ Burchard of Worms, Yvo of Chartres, and Gratian give, on this subject, basically

the same text: see, for example: Yvo, *Decreti pars IV, De festivis et ieiuniis*, etc., c. 63, *P.L.* 161. 277D.

[30] P. Guignard, *Les monuments primitifs de la Règle cistercienne*, Dijon, 1878, c. 41, p. 129. On all these points the person who is the most knowledgeable on Cistercian liturgy, Fr. C. Waddell, has given me information for which I am grateful.

[31] This is an antiphonary which is conserved today at Westmalle Abbey. The text prior to 1147 is found in the manuscript, Berlin, Lat., Oct. 402, attributed to St. Stephen Harding. The later text is to be found in several manuscripts, such as the one at Westmalle, studied by J. Pothier, 'Antienne "Anima mea liquefacta est"', *Revue du chant grégorien*, 18 (1909), pp. 3–12.

[32] Cf. Dom Capelle, 'La liturgie mariale en Occident', in *Maria*, Paris, 1949, p. 228.

[33] Cf. *Recueil d'études*, I, pp. 188–90.

[34] Conrad of Hirsau, *Dialogus super auctores*, ed. R. B. C. Huygens, Leyden, 1970, pp. 84–6.

[35] p. 74.

[36] p. 113.

[37] p. 115.

[38] p. 86.

[39] pp. 111–12.

[40] p. 112.

[41] pp. 1261–3.

[42] p. 113.

[43] pp. 116–17.

[44] p. 114.

[45] p. 56.

[46] p. 73.

[47] Ed. in *Un maître de la vie spirituelle au XIe siècle, Jean de Fécamp*, Paris, 1946, p. 185.

[48] Gen. 34:1–31.

[49] *Un maître . . .*, p. 191.

[50] Ibid., p. 192. 157. The example of Dinah is also quoted by St. Bernard, as a symbol of 'curiosity' in his treatise *On the Steps of Humility and Pride*, no. 29, ed. *S. Bernardi opera*, III, p. 39, and in a decree of the council of Reims in 1157 on the enclosure of nuns, quoted by R. Gazeau, 'La clôture des moniales au XIIe siècle en France', *Revue Mabillon*, 58 (1970–5), pp. 298 and 307.

[51] Ed. F. S. Schmitt, *S. Anselmi opera*, III, Edinburgh, 1946, pp. 80–3.

[52] Ibid., p. 80, in the apparatus.

[53] p. 80. 19.

[54] p. 80. 23.

[55] p. 81. 33.

[56] p. 83. 111.

[57] Ed. B. Bischoff and B. Taeger, *Johannis Mantuani in Cantica et de S. Maria Tractatus ad comitissam Matildam*, Fribourg, 1973.

[58] A list is given in ibid., p. 3.

[59] Ibid., pp. 25–6.

[60] Ibid., p. 28; the editors suggest, in the apparatus, 'that it is possible that it is a question of the feast of the Purification'. But, as we saw above, the liturgy of the Assumption had, since its introduction into the West, made use of texts from the Song. On this connection between the Assumption and the idea that Mary was contemplative and active, cf. *Vie religieuse et vie contemplative*, Paris, 1969, pp. 265–70.

[61] p. 29.

[62] p. 25.

[63] p. 155.

[64] p. 30.

[65] p. 29, 'Salomon voluit Cantica pluraliter proferre'.

[66] *Vita S. Iulianae*, n. 6, *A. Sanct. Boll.*, Aprilis I, ed. Antwerp, 1675, p. 446; n. 26, p. 453.

[67] Lambert of Ardres, *Chronicles of the Counts of Guines*, ed. *MGH, SS* 24, p. 598.

[68] The manuscript of Le Mans has been edited by C. E. Pickford, *The Song of Songs. A Twelfth-Century French Version, edited from ms. 173 of the Bibliothèque Municipale of Le Mans*, Oxford, 1974. In a further study on the language of love in the twelfth century, I hope to develop what is suggested here on the sources of this paraphrase and on the attitude of Church authorities towards the vernacular translations of the Song.

[69] The merited admiration and the influence of St. Bernard's *Sermons on the Song* are witnessed to by the very numerous manuscripts which have come down to us—for the first century after their redaction (*S. Bernardi opera*, I, Rome, 1957, p. xxiii) and a much greater number of later witnesses—as well as the vast and varied literature which they provoked very early on: *Recueil d'études*, I, pp. 176-90 and 350-1. The influence of the Song on current monastic literature is illustrated, for example, by the letter written by an anonymous monk published by R. M. Thomson, 'A Twelfth Century Letter from Bury St. Edmunds Abbey', *Revue bénédictine*, 82 (1972), pp. 87-97: the editor has identified several citations or reminiscences of the Song; and there are still more. It is revealing that from the Song, quoted more frequently, it is the fundamental themes which are borrowed, whereas from Ovid the author takes merely stylistic embellishments.

[70] Ed. F. Gastaldelli, *Goffredo di Auxerre. Expositio in Cantica Canticorum*, Rome, 1974, 2 vols.; p. 17 cites Col. 2: 3.

[71] p. 27.

[72] p. 41.

[73] p. 44.

[74] p. 34.

[75] p. 48.

[76] p. 113.

[77] p. 115.

[78] p. 187.

[79] p. 250.

[80] p. 283.

[81] pp. 283-98.

[82] pp. 309-10.

[83] p. 322.

[84] pp. 340-4.

[85] p. 380.

[86] p. 438.

[87] pp. 461-3.

[88] p. 460.

[89] p. 461.

[90] pp. 459-60.

[91] pp. 503-24.

[92] pp. 532-8.

[93] The same sort of interpretation is found, for example, in the commentary in verse (*Expositio metrica*) in the manuscript Reims 1275, fos. 137v-146v, incl.: Quem sitio vobis nunc oscula porrigat oris . . . ; for example, on *iunctura femorum*, fo. 144, etc.

[94] The Commentary of Geoffrey takes up, in Gastaldelli's edition, 601 pages; the Indices extend to p. 668. Thus the indications given here agree with the fact that, when the description of feminine beauty appears in twelfth-century literature, it does so out-

side monasticism, as has been shown by D. S. Brewer, 'The Ideal of Feminine Beauty in Medieval Literature, especially "Harley Lyrics", Chaucer and some Elizabethans', *Medieval Literary Review*, 50 (1955), pp. 257–68; and even in this non-monastic literature we find a few descriptive elements from the Song: cf. ibid., p. 257, n. 3.

IV

Another Master in the Art of Loving: Ovid

1. *Cicero, forerunner to Ovid*

BEFORE we speak of Ovid, we must recall that there was another great writer of classical antiquity who influenced monastic love literature in a way which, though it was limited, was, even so, decisive. This was Cicero. For it is within the framework of the ideas which he handed down to posterity that certain formulas from Ovid have been received.

Both these authors were the objects of introductions called *accessus*, so named because they gave access to texts and equipped readers for interpreting them. Such literature is less abundant and of later date for Cicero than for Ovid. This is probably due to the fact that there seemed less necessity for it, since it was easier and more natural to read the pagan moralist Cicero with a Christian interpretation than was possible for the immoralist, Ovid. When the *accessus* to Cicero's works began to come out, they dealt with his treatise *On Friendship*, *De Amicitia*.[1] But monastic writers, even before the publication of these *accessus*, started borrowing ideas or formulas linked with this form of love of God and man which we call friendship.

It has now been established for certain, and with precision, that in the twenty-five passages of his treatise *On the Necessity of Loving God*, in his Letters, and his *Sermons on the Song*, St. Bernard of Clairvaux quotes fifteen terms or formulas from Cicero's treatise.[2] This is true in particular for 'pure love',[3] which corresponds to the disinterested love mentioned by

Cicero.[4] The Ciceronian idea of 'friendship which is not based on the hope of recompense'[5] is to be found in St. Bernard's writings.[6] The most important idea that he received from Cicero, and which is to be seen continually in his works, is precisely that of friendship which asks for nothing back in return, a love which has no other result except love itself.[7]

However, Bernard never merely copies another author: he takes inspiration from him and becomes, as it were, an extension of him. He reinterprets, and, if necessary, Christianizes him. For example, the word 'charity' was already to be found in Cicero; but since it was also in the New Testament, Bernard did not need to look to Cicero. However, the idea that friendship does away with social barriers by establishing an equality between friends of different social conditions was another matter. Bernard took up this theme and transformed it, going a step further. He suggests that friendship makes two beings not only 'equal', but 'one'. When dealing with the foundation of friendship, Bernard substitutes 'love of God' for the Ciceronian 'Virtue', and in this way he replaces a pagan concept with a Christian reality.

This limited but real influence of Cicero on St. Bernard is not apparent in his Letter 11 on love, which dates probably from 1124 or 1125. But it is very evident in the treatise *On the Necessity of Loving God*, written somewhere between 1126 and 1141. It is also to be found in nine Letters, one of which at least dates from 1124;[8] and it appears also in the *Sermons on the Song*. We can say, then, that it is one of the constants of his whole work.

Now, Abelard, even before 1121, the date of the condemnation of his *Introduction to Theology*, had written of friendship and taken his inspiration from Cicero's treatise *On Invention*. It is possible that Bernard, in his treatise *On the Necessity of Loving God*, wished to oppose Abelard, and in particular his commentary on the Letter to the Romans. In order to do this, he had to read Cicero's treatise *On Friendship*, with the result stressed by an expert in these terms: 'There is more and greatly deeper material from Cicero in Bernard than in Abelard.'[9] There is no doubt but that the Ciceronian idea of pure love was to be found in the writings of St. Augustine and St. Ambrose, whose works were in the library at Clairvaux.[10] It is also equally sure that Bernard went back to their common source, and in this way gave a definitive impetus to a whole school of thought which was to develop after his times. Aelred of Rievaulx, in the decade which followed the death of his master Bernard, completed the Christianizing of Cicero's treatise *On Friendship* in his own work, whose very title, *On Spiritual Friendship*, is inspired by Cicero. What Bernard had been content merely to suggest, in his own way, poet and genius and initiator that he was, was taken up by Aelred and exposed more systematically. And it is within the framework of these conceptions that we can place certain Ovidian elements.

II. *The Ovidian complex*

Ovid was cited in both monastic and secular love literature. But, in the first group especially, he inevitably roused psychological and spiritual problems because of the diversity of his work with its inherent qualities and dangers.

As we remarked in reference to Solomon, so also we can say that there were several Ovids: the scientific Ovid who exposed the facts of natural history in his *Metamorphoses*;[11] the rhetorician, poet, and master in the art of writing who merited to be taken as a model in this domain; the moralist, on condition of his advice on practical wisdom being sifted out from his works; and even Ovid the theologian, on condition of examining his works on ancient mythology with a view to finding the sense that they could have for Christians; and finally, there was the erotic Ovid who offered—for those who wanted them—recipes for getting more sensual pleasure out of life.[12] All these elements were intermingled not only in his work but also in the use which was made of it. Rarely in the texts do we find a single one of these different Ovids purely distinct. Furthermore, each Ovid could be taken literally, with or without humour, or used to embellish the style of writings containing ideas quite alien to his own. It was also even possible to transpose him, more or less, and at different levels. Such is the origin of that vast amount of literature of the 'moralized Ovid' which is constantly being studied by historians. In addition to all these Ovids, more or less legitimately sprung from the authentic Ovid, there were pseudo-Ovids. They were often later, but at least one of them, the *Facetus* of Aurigeno, is now recognized as dating from the second half of the twelfth century.[13]

The Ovidian corpus drew the attention of the authors of the *accessus* earlier on than did the works of Cicero.[14] This was because Ovid fascinated by the beauty of his verse; and yet, at the same time, he was perceived to be dangerous on account of the inherent paganism and eroticism. We notice then that he causes a psychological phenomenon similar to that which had appeared, in many generations of monks, in connection with Origen, a phenomenon which we can typify as something of a complex.[15] On the one hand he was necessary, and yet, on the other, people were warned about the perils associated with his reputation. This instinctive repression with regard to Origen had been shaken off by looking for statements in the Christian tradition which legitimized his teaching. But for Ovid this resource was not available. So the problem had to be solved in another way.

The easiest one was to purge his writings. It is now established that, in the text known to the middle ages, certain lines had been altered, probably on the basis of an archetype from which all other copies were made.[16] But that was not enough. Even modified in this way and literally corrupted, these texts, and especially certain among them, remained very dangerous. So young scholars were warned against reading them: at Paris, towards the end of the twelfth century, Alexander Neckham recommended adolescent youths not to read these 'love poems'. In the manuscripts of several miscellanies, certain extracts from Ovid were eliminated.[17] And those which were left were submitted to a real exegetical study using the same processes as for the allegorical interpretation of Holy Scripture.[18] Some even went so far as to make out that Ovid was a Christian—not even an anonymous Christian (who does not know whether he is); and people were inventive in finding in his texts matter for re-enforcing, en-lightening Christian aspirations. Hidden meanings were dis-covered in his writings, and his heroes became models: Myrrha was the symbol of Mary; Bacchus and Aeneas symbolized Christ.[19] Later on, a pious Franciscan went so far as to 'dedicate, certainly without malice, his copy of *Remedies to Love* to the glory of the Virgin Mary, whose feast fell on the next day'.[20] Thus, for Ovid as for Origen, there was a whole scale of attitudes, from the most hostile to the most admiring. But whereas for Origen it was the positive elements which counted most, the readers of Ovid more often than not had bad consciences, even though they might not go so far as to feel inhibited. The reaction to Ovid varies from one milieu to another, from one person to another.

III. *Ovid and monks*

To a certain extent we can say that there was a monastic Cicero and a monastic Seneca. It was of the latter that William of Saint-Thierry could say, 'He is one of ours: *Seneca noster*'.[21] Was this also true of Ovid? It does not seem so. In traditional monasticism of the first half of the twelfth century, Conrad of Hirsau in his *Dialogue on the Authors* was very severe about him.[22] On the other hand, Baudri, abbot of Bourgueil who be-came bishop of Dole, went to the other extreme not only in imitating Ovid, but also in taking great pains to defend him when he was reproached for having corrupted Roman youth and so deserving to be exiled. But this was 'in all respects, an excep-tion'.[23] Moreover, this poet, more worldly than deeply religious, is not a witness of monastic love literature.

But among those writers who are witnesses to this literature the first in chronological order, William of Saint-Thierry, thought fit in 1119 or 1120 to write a real anti-Ovidian work. His treatise *On the Nature and Dignity of Love* contains a section entitled 'About false love and the doctors who teach it.' In this text William declares open warfare against Ovid, and it must be cited within a fairly wide context:

Love, as we have shown, is given naturally by the author of nature to the human soul. But, because man has lost the law of God, he must be educated and learn to purify love, and learn to love truly; he must learn to progress and how to set about this: he must learn to grow strong and the way to do so.

For shameful carnal love had its masters in the past who taught its depraved practices. These men expended great skill, and were so successful in corrupting themselves and others, that the doctor of the Art of Loving, himself, was constrained by the lovers and companions of his depravities to change, as it were, his tune, and retract in part what he had all too indecently sung. He was obliged to write *Remedia Amoris*, he who had once written about the fires kindled by carnal love, even though it was burning already within him and his disciples without any constraint, not only reviving the age-old spurs of love but also inventing new ones.

Doubtless, this man did not set out to teach the art of unbridling carnal love, even though it was burning within him and his disciples, without any constraint imposed by reason. But, desiring to rule such love by rules which supersede all other rules, he led it to wantonness, and by untimely stimulation he pushed it to the folly of lechery.

In these depraved and perverted men indeed, the vice of carnal desire, going beyond all bounds, ruined the order of nature. Their minds ought, according to the normal order of nature, to have been carried by their own weight, by the love that was in them, upwards towards God who created them. But, dragged down by the captivating charms of the flesh, they failed to understand, and set themselves alongside the brute beasts, becoming like to them. They ranked themselves with those of whom it is said: 'My spirit does not remain in these men, for they are flesh. . . .'[24]

Even in his denunciation William softened the severity of his judgement and endeavoured to excuse Ovid, who surely did not intend to do evil. Even so, the condemnation remains. Now this influenced other writers, for example a secular poet such as Macabru, as has been more than once observed.[25] It also influenced St. Bernard, whom we know to have read, and commented on before his monks, William's treatise where this passage is found.[26] It was more than a warning. William attacks not only the eroticism in Ovid's licentious verses, but also the underlying conception of man and his relations with God. This false theology needs refuting more than condemning and it is just this that Bernard and William do. Bernard does not even take the trouble to denounce Ovid: was it timely? He constructs a theology based on and entirely contrary conception of the image of God in man, and this he does partly by commenting on another love poet, Solomon. Such solid teaching was the best antidote, one which was more effective than any interpolation, paraphrase, or declaration of warfare.

Paradoxically—and this is a sign of admirable freedom—in order to expose his Christian anthropology, Bernard is not afraid to call upon Ovid as an 'authority', for he pointed out man's superiority over brute beasts since he alone 'was created with his head raised heavenwards and a sublime visage able to gaze at the heavens'.[27] True, this quotation, found several times in Bernard, is taken from the *Metamorphoses*.[28] In one case, even, it is immediately followed by a verse from Holy Scripture exalting the greatness of man, and all that follows merely develops the poet's theme in the light of other quotations from the Bible.[29] Elsewhere it serves to evoke the Christian's aspiration towards 'his blessed and eternal home'.[30] And it is a reminiscence of this same formula which sets the tone for Bernard's great doctrinal discourse on man's 'rectification' which remedies the fact that he is bowed down, bent towards earth because he is a sinner. In this context the idea suggested by Ovid is used to explain one word found in Solomon's Song in the passage where it says that the 'upright' have the privilege of knowing how to love.[31] Further on, in the same explanation of the same love song, the 'poet' is again quoted, and this time with praise, as having spoken 'elegantly and beautifully'. In this instance, Bernard is certainly dependent on an anthology.[32] The *Metamorphoses* were not one of his primary sources, Ovid was here again more of an authority whose witness is immediately confirmed by St. Paul's. Thus, in many ways, Ovid the theologian corrected the erotic Ovid and furnished arguments against himself. The language or idea might well come from him originally, but the doctrine exposed in connection with Solomon was that of the Apostle and other authentic interpreters of Christian love. And it is confirmed today by an anthropologist like E. Straus, who analyses the meaning of the 'upright posture of man, which is to be born to see, bound to behold'. 'Man's very body structure reveals his contemplative orientation. With the upright posture a particular mode of being in the world is simultaneously given. This mode is contemplative in its foundations, for the upright posture enables man to take a distance from things and thus to see them in themselves. And seeing things in themselves is the foundation for a contemplative way of vision. By contrasting the animal eye with the human eye, Straus reveals the specifically contemplative dimensions of human vision.'[33] Thus, it is of no importance that Bernard, and sometimes, more frequently than he, monastic authors such as Aelred, Geoffrey of Auxerre, Gilbert of Hoyland, occasionally borrowed embellishing quotations from Ovid. At Clairvaux even, in the second half of the twelfth century, an anthology of *Extracts on Love* contains passages from eight of Ovid's works, but in these passages we find only ethical precepts or 'common-sense' remarks. This is particularly so for nine verses taken from the *Art of Loving* and the sole verse from the Remedies.[34] The main effect that the reading of Ovid had on monasticism was to contribute to the appearance of quite another literature and to incite authors to frequent Solomon's school. Ovid was a stimulus: the dangers found in his *Art of Loving* were remedied by the Song of Songs.

IV. *The secular's Ovid*

It would seem that everything has been written about the medieval Ovid, yet research work is still going on, and is producing some results. For a long time the research concerned the influence that certain passages had on other medieval works, but today, on the whole, what is mainly being studied is the literary transmission and the chronology of Ovidian texts—whether or not they are authentic—and the mentality with which the reading of the witnesses was approached. It is indeed difficult to appreciate exactly the importance of Ovid. It has greatly varied, according to different milieux and people, and its long and tormented history extends far beyond the spatio-temporal confines of twelfth-century France.

Within twelfth-century France, we must first distinguish several manners of using Ovid. Particularly before his works began to be translated, in the second half of the century, students could amuse themselves by reading them more or less clandestinely, with a more or less good conscience. It is possible that the official prohibitions merely increased the attraction of the forbidden fruit. This use of Ovid has left scarcely any trace in manuscripts. Others studied him with an end to their own literary formation, and even their moral education. Certain even went so far as to teach Ovid solely for this purpose: this is clearly pointed out in a distinction made by Peter the Chanter.[35] Finally, Ovid's influence on writers varies from one to another, and it is not at all evident that it always made them turn aside from the norms which were part of their own vocation or the society to which they belonged. Chrétien de Troyes, whom we know for certain had read Ovid, and even translated him, did not, for all that, become immoral.

It was from 1160 onward that he translated into French certain *Ovidiana*, but their contents are unknown to us since they are no longer extant. In his works, as in the anonymous *Aeneas* and various other romances which proved to be his own, it has been possible to pick out many ideas and formulas, which though they came from Ovid—as well as from many another ancient poet[36]— were founded upon thought of Christian inspiration. The first French Ovid which has come down to us is worth examining apart, and this we shall do shortly, for it is revealing of all that such a text could suggest: it is an adaptation of his *Art of Loving*. Apart from translations and adaptations of this kind, this poem served as a model for a whole series of French works with the same title. They are generally didactic in nature and deliver precepts, moral or otherwise.[37] But in the twelfth century they still leave wide room for fantasy, a sort of ironical play on mytho-

logical facts: even the gods—who are known not to have existed—
are supposed to have had loves similar to man's, and sometimes
worse than man's! With the development of scholasticism,
during the thirteenth century, these writings were sometimes
systematized to the point of being serious, even boring. Later
still, when they came out of the schools, they became more and
more licentious.

A good example of the humour with which a twelfth-century
cleric from Champagne played with Ovid is seen in a work by
Andreas Capellanus (Andrew the Chaplain) which has recently
come to be regarded more as a piece of irony than a serious witness to real morals.[38] This long bantering work—we could call it
a farce—uses feigned gravity which has led many a historian
astray. Such art was perhaps even too refined to have great
success: the manuscripts of the text are few and far between, and
more than a hundred years had to pass before it was translated
first into French, and then into other languages.[39]

In many authors we can discern less an explicit reference to
Ovid than spontaneously occurring reminiscences of formulas
taken from his writings and those of Holy Scripture. Moreover,
reminiscences of Ovid are far fewer than those from the Bible.
Such scholastic memories could bear on themes, symbols, and
linguistic expressions of love common to many different literatures, and are found among the monks as much as among
seculars. These will be dealt with in a forthcoming work.[40]

Lastly, some writers gave themselves to consciously imitating
Ovid, and the first example is offered by the romance *Pyramus
and Thisbe*, the two lovers who thought they were to be eternally
separated by death, and who, one after the other, commit
suicide with the same dagger, while the white fruits of a mulberry
tree, splashed with blood, turn black.[41] This tale, so innocent and
charming, which via the East had found its way into Ovid—
especially his *Metamorphoses*—in the course of its meanderings
entered medieval Western literature, mingled with elements
handed down from classical Latinity.[42] There we find harmoni-
ously and pleasantly united the fantasy of play with a great deal

of legend and allegory and the seriousness of an epic and moral narration, in the course of which Christian precepts are acknowledged even though they may sometimes be infringed. These two elements combine with the mixture of happiness and suffering which is found in every human existence, with the combat it entails, the 'militia' required for any victory over self and circumstances: antagonism between life and death, love and separation. These are all so many themes which, let it be remarked, are also found in the Song of Songs.

We have a glimpse of the variety of forms in which the medieval Ovid could be clothed. But it is not enough to notice that he existed. The question is what did medieval people look for in Ovid that they did not find in other authors. It could hardly be details concerning erotic activity. In a mainly rural society, even for people born in the towns, there was always the nearby spectacle of the way animals behave, either in stables or in fields. Then, habitation favoured such promiscuity that even the most intimate amatory behaviour could be heard or seen by the youngest of children: there was no need to read books for initiation. And even in the *Art of Loving*, details concerning the life of love were mingled with such long considerations that those who were looking for something else could only be bored.

What the writers did find in Ovid was, first of all, aphorisms with which to embellish their own works. Some such formulas have been picked out among Cistercian works. There were also some such definitions to be found in every troubadour and trouvère. There we find literary maxims willingly accepted from this master in the art of writing; moral sentences which could be applied to love, even, and especially perhaps, to faithful love. This can be seen in cases like Folquet of Marseilles, for whom we have a precise repertory of quotations which very often are nothing more than sentences of a very general kind.[43] Truly, there was nothing in Ovid, at least in the twelfth century, to corrupt public morals.

Next, it should be noticed that the *Metamorphoses* are used at least as often as the *Art of Loving* and the *Remedies*. Now they contain, in relation with the love of the gods, vast mythological material, serving as psychological models, or, as we would say today, 'archetypes' common to every human tradition, and recognized in contemporary situations. More than ideas, these writings offered food for the imagination, a stimulus for poetic creation, materials, and, if not a method, at least suggestions for analysing sentiments. It was in no way a return to the past— neither to that of the poet himself, nor to that of Eastern sources —but rather a means of interpreting and expressing, with fantasy and refreshingly, the problems which medieval love experiences raised. Save for exceptional cases, there was nothing of a teaching on love, but merely a poetic play in which writers were careful not to take Ovid any more seriously than he probably had taken himself. But this artist had been so creative of beauty that it was this, and not the poison his works contained, that came to the fore, not only in his work, but also in the interest which was shown in him. The humour with which he was read and quoted appears in particular in the discovered and exploited contrast between the majesty of these so-called divinities and their paltry conduct. Ovid, on the whole, was not a source of immorality: there was no way of committing sin which had to be learned from him. More often than not, even in the description of sins recognized as such, and in the judgement of them, reference was made to the more moral parts of his writings. Moreover, he had the monopoly neither of these riches come down from the past, nor of the contrast established between the great heroes and the passions to which they gave themselves by day and by night, nor even of the precepts of good conduct and the just appreciation of human situations. All these elements were to be found also in Virgil, Statius, Propertius, Catullus, and many others. But the frequent resort to such poets greatly contributed to the refinement of the style and thought of the authors of secular writings on love. And, after all, it was a partly similar arsenal of beautiful formulas, poetic images, and insights into the deep psychology of men and women which the monks in

particular, but others too, though to a lesser extent, also sought
for in the Song of Songs.

v. *The French Ovid*

The first French translation of Ovid which has come down to us
has recently been edited.[44] Thus it has become more accessible
to study, which is most useful. This text is slightly later than the
twelfth century, the golden age of monastic love literature. The
first two books date from the beginning of the thirteenth century;
the third book, which will not be considered here, is a later one.
Monks, as we have seen, were not totally unacquainted with
Ovid, but they had not taken the trouble to translate him. They
had another and more widely diffused love literature in the Song
and its commentaries. Indeed this French Ovid was not to have
great success. There are only four extant manuscripts—even less
than for Andreas Capellanus—and they are all of the fifteenth
century. However, the text is worth considering. It will allow us
to grasp how certain Christian medieval milieux reacted to a
pagan's ancient poem on the *Art of Loving*. As for the French
Solomon, the most ancient French text of Ovid is not a mere
translation: it is, if not an imitation like so many others, at least
an adaptation, partly abridged, partly paraphrased. Especially, it
is to be noticed, the poem is preceded by an introduction—an
accessus—and accompanied with glosses, and it is perhaps these
additions which are more important than the poem itself, for our
purposes here, because of what they show us of medieval psychology. These commentaries are inspired by court literature and by
popular songs called 'carols'; so it is that we find there a pastoral,
two rounds, varied refrains, some of which are stamped with a
fairly vulgar eroticism or 'strongly tinged with anti-feminism':[45]
this last trait is common to Ovid and many witnesses to secular
love literature. The mixture of chivalric ideas, and statements
made by the 'villeins',[46] confirms the difference of social milieux
and the writings in which they delighted. The glosses also bring
out certain of the moral and courteous implications[47] of reading

Ovid. They sometimes quote Holy Scripture, including, though rarely, the Song.

From the introduction onwards, a distinction is made among those who are acquainted with the art of loving; they are classified according to the social categories to which they belong: 'young birds', both men and women, know this art by 'nature'—the very environment into which they are born prepares them for it; poor people, villeins and knaves, know this art from practice. As to the clerics, they have 'learnt' it in narrations and books: it is admitted that they do not generally have experience of it. If, afterwards, we go through the glosses, which constitute the specifically medieval element, it is noticed that woman is always judged in relation to man and the pleasure which he can get out of her, and not for herself, with consideration for the pleasure which might be hers. By developing in detail certain allusions to Graeco-Roman mythology, which, though they were understood by Ovid's first readers, were not so in medieval times, the glosses always attribute unfaithfulness, fickleness, and craving to women, not to men. God is mentioned too, for example in a carol on the death of love:

> You who will see her, for God, say:
> Death has got hold of me, unless
> she have mercy on me.[48]

This recalls the Song. But a little further on a verse from the Song is quoted: 'Come, my lady, come and thou shalt drink.'[49] In this way the Song was used for commenting on Ovid, just as certain monks quoted Ovid in their commentaries on the Song, for the simple reason that there are—as will be seen[50]—themes common to all love literature. In the same way the chambermaid or the servant in Ovid[51] lead one to think of the young maidens who, in the Song, are 'friends of the bride'. The pun about uncomprehending reading being a negation of reading, taken from the Distichs attributed to Cato, had already been exploited by monks in connection with reading about God, *lectio divina*. This is here applied to the reading of Ovid.[52] The author of the translation and the glosses is manifestly familiar with the Christian tradition: he names God, and establishes an analogy between prayer addressed to God and that which a lover makes to his lady-love.[53]

And yet, within these common cultural elements, the whole trend of the work is profoundly different from that of the commentaries on the Song. Here room is given to anger, jealousy,[54] and even to certain very vulgar ways of taking revenge.[55] The sole aim is always pleasure: the 'joy of love' is taken in its most sensual meaning. Never do we find mention of disinterestedness, affection, friendship, whereas for Christians the fleshly union between husband and wife is a form of friendship. If what the Book of Genesis says about God, or if other biblical facts are recalled as moralizing elements, it is always in the very Ovidian sense of the maximum gratification. When the lover 'joins his hands', prays to his lady, he speaks to her of God. Ovid also spoke of the gods; here the gloss puts this word with a capital letter, and we have the passage from god to God which is degradation, the reduction of the Christian notion of God, rather than its elevation, its sublimation. Ovid always supposes that these gods existed: 'It is greatly profitable that the gods should exist because it is a must that we should create them,' says he: these gods are Jupiter, Juno, Venus, and others, and the glossator does not deny this.[56] Yet he believes in the God of his faith, his religion, and his culture, and so there is constant confusion in his text,[57] which doubtless we must be careful neither to exaggerate nor to dramatize. He distinguished between his faith and his literary play, he was able to choose in the Bible what served his purpose for the moment. From Solomon, for example, he borrowed a very pejorative judgement about women: 'And concerning what we have just said, that there are no, or very few, loyal women, Solomon mentions it in Scripture, where he says, "Who will find a friendly woman?"; as he openly says: "There is not one." '[58] Thus from the beginning to the end there is a constant mingling of biblism, of immorality, and a minimum of Christian ethics. No enthusiasm, little joy: only pleasure.

As to the very sensual and yet so very refined descriptions of the play of love, the glossator does not insist:[59] he takes it for granted that they are clear enough, and so they are. It is in one of these passages that he again mentions God, as a banal exclamation, not a prayer:

> God! I cannot sleep at night,
> The sickness of love awakes me![60]

We can guess that his spontaneous reactions are Christian, whereas his cultural refinement is Ovidian. He is truly of his times; he sometimes transposes Ovid into medieval popular carols. He can be an extremely vulgar realist, but that is rare, more so than in the fabliaux; he does, however, quote a refrain taken from one of the most obscene ones.[61] On the whole, the refinement of this French Ovid is situated between the elevated level of certain romances, and the more down-to-earth level of popular stories.

One of the most constant attitudes of this author—and he shares it in common with the majority of witnesses to secular love literature—is the scorn of women.[62] If this attitude is to be found in minor, often anonymous and generally later texts of medieval monasticism,[63] it is absent among the great minds such as Peter Damian,[64] Bernard of Clairvaux, in the commentaries of the Song,[65] and in songs written by St. Hildegard, where lofty images of Mary, New Eve, and of the Church, Bride of Christ leave no room for speaking evil of woman as such.[66] It is true that we are dealing here with a practical rather than a doctrinal anti-feminism, contrary to what we find in Abelard, for example, whose speculative depreciation of womankind[67] goes hand in hand with a strong attraction, and even a real esteem, for women in general or one woman in particular.[68] Here, the dominant note is practical distrust with regard to the failings of womankind: to the fickleness, the faithlessness we have already quoted is added, in a much more general way, her 'malice'.[69] So, says the glossator, this translation of Ovid must not get into female hands;[70] the privilege of using the wiles of the art of loving is reserved for men only: women would make use of it against them. Male pleasure comes first in this 'stag' literature written for men who use women with a sometimes very far-pushed cynicism.[71] There is a proverb which Bernard had applied to angels and men: these latter being likened to those 'little dogs' whom the Gospel says eat the crumbs fallen from their master's table.[72] Here this proverb is put into the mouth of a villein: 'He who loves me, loves my dog.' Now this saying, in the present context, is simply applied to women, reduced to the condition of a dog in the crudest way possible.[73]

This is altogether a strange association of Ovid's gods and the Creator God of Christian belief; of a conception of nature as being a set of drives which may all be legitimately satisfied to satiation point, and a reminiscence of the idea of sin![74] What a long way there is between this lack of morality, justified by Ovid, and the way of 'following nature', by controlling it, liberating it from sin, expounded by William of Saint-Thierry.[75] Here there is nothing at all left of Christian ethics, even though the faith from which it is derived may still be underlying. Part of the vocabulary of Christian ascesis has even crept in here: the maxim 'know thyself' handed down by Ovid and Apollo had already been commented upon by St. Bernard as a means to humility. An interpretation which was not to be found in Ovid is here introduced: 'Whoever knows himself, little esteems himself.'[76] But it is without consequence. Elsewhere, an element of biblical morality—the warning against sodomites—is also added to Ovid.[77] We even have a quotation from the Gospels, and another from St. Paul.[78]

In short, the French Ovid offers us a curious mixture of Christian facts—which are occasionally little more than cultural adornments—and pagan influence consciously received and accepted. We notice that the glossator approves all the erotic refinement of the Ovidian poem, which increases as it approaches the end. And he even then adds a few indications which are more realistic and precise than those in the original text.[79] And yet, with all that, there is sometimes a surprising reserve in the language employed. Such reserve makes us think of taboos and inhibitions which could almost be believed to be modern.[80] There is nothing really perverse in all that, because, together with a certain degradation of Ovid's refinements to the level of popular love, for example in the carols, there is also a certain raising of Ovid's sensuality to the level of courtly love in all its most noble manifestations. The glossator says of Ovid, 'What he wants to prove is that to make love with love is a good manner of labouring. For as he says here and elsewhere, it is chivalry in arms which helps to conquest, and this chivalry of love is a help to maintaining the other.'[81] In this text which is so full of both realism and literary allegory we must distinguish between love as a sentiment, and that ensemble of sensations which go to make up sensual love pleasure: it is more often the latter which is presented in the French Ovid. The proportion is the inverse in the Song, and this rapid perusal of the French Ovid helps us to measure the immense contrast there is between him and the love song attributed to Solomon.

VI. *Pagan writings and Holy Scripture*

There existed, because of the Song, a biblical art of loving; and because of Ovid there was also a non-biblical art of loving. But even this was not read without the Bible. The pleasure to be found in the reading of pagan authors did not exclude a scriptural cultural background, nor did it stifle all Christian reactions. The French Ovid has shown us how the ancient poet was translated and commented on during the Christian middle ages. Another text which has now been edited gives a precise example of the way in which he was, in fact, assimilated. This text is that of the *Letters of Two Lovers*, written somewhere between the Île de France and the region of Clairvaux, in the second half of the twelfth century, and, more precisely, so it seems, between 1183 and 1185. The manuscript is made up of extracts from a no-longer-extant larger set of letters really exchanged between two people and which probably, to start with, were just little notes of affection.[82] The two people who 'court by correspondence', designated by the initials *V* from *Vir*, man, and *M* from *Mulier*, woman, are a cleric, who does not seem to have been a monk, and a partner, of whom we cannot tell whether she was a nun, a canoness, or a secular. The last seems to be the most probable. Between the two it seems that there was a relationship of master to pupil similar to that which existed, at the beginning at least, between Abelard and Héloïse: a friendship which is neither entirely spiritual nor entirely carnal. There are some clear allusions to the desires arising from the flesh on the man's part. Yet neither the vocabulary nor the ideas ever go very far in this sense. Room is made for 'probity' and for 'virtue'. The two correspondents speak now of 'love', now of 'friendship', and style themselves alternately as lover and beloved, as friend and friend, with a shift from the more familiar 'thou' to 'you', which is used by the man as to some strange and distant lady. We have here an amusement between lettered persons, which has its own particular charm, on the theme of love from afar.

What, we may ask, are the inspirational sources? Holy Scripture is the most abundantly cited; about ten verses from the Song are used;[83] and in particular the idea of the 'sickness of love' borrowed from the Song and not from Ovid.[84] Allusion is made to a formula from St. Paul about what each partner in the conjugal couple 'owes' to the other.[85] Moral proverbs are, in reality, phrases from Scripture.[86] God is often named, and the atmosphere in which the two correspondents live and think is strongly impregnated with Christian religion; it is even that which restrains them from going further than epistolary relations in their union.

At the same time, a definition of love—which applies equally to carnal union and spiritual union—is borrowed from Cicero.[87] Horace and other classical writers are also present. But by far the most used—and more so by the man (thirty-four times) than by the woman (eighteen times)—is Ovid, especially in his *Metamorphoses* (eighteen times); occasionally the *Fasti*, the *Epistles*, the *Amores*, the *Tristia*, the *Art of Loving*, and the

Remedies are also put to contribution. Certain of the Fathers of the Church are known, as is Boethius. We have proof of a very fine culture, especially in the man. And we can truly say that pagan texts and Holy Scripture, Ovid and Solomon, are in no way mutually exclusive in the authors of this minor document representing an intermediary between the love of possession and enjoyment extolled by Ovid and the love of the spiritual search taught by the commentators of the Song.

Thus there is a great variety of levels in the experience of love. On the whole, we may say that these were situated between two poles symbolized by Solomon and Ovid. In monastic literature the Song is much more important than Ovid; in secular literature Ovid holds first place. Both were poetic works offering food for the imagination in similar ways: there are as many 'metamorphoses' in the Song as in Ovid. In the former, women appear successively as servant, princess, sister, fiancée, bride. And Solomon is now king, now shepherd, now hunter. These images all lent themselves to poetic use in both instances, to varying extents. Solomon and Ovid were deeply ingrained in the culture of the times.

But without any doubt the two love literatures are very clearly separated by the distinctly differing moral direction taken by each one. This explains the priority given to either Solomon or Ovid. In order to evaluate the loftiness of the Song, it is enough to compare it with the *Art of Loving*. We at once see that this work favours sensuality, whereas in the Song this factor is not evident unless pointed out. It is understandable that monks did not see it. If there is any eroticism, it is of a chaste nature. The poem sings the praises of fidelity tested by separation. In Ovid, to the contrary, everything tends to 'consummation'—an obsession which is in no way dissimulated. The Song has nothing of the crude and detailed realism of Ovid's poems; it merely alludes to what Ovid and his glossator state quite openly. Readers who wanted sensual satisfaction knew very well which author to choose. Ovid, by an effect of contrasts, helps to appreciate the chastity of the Song. And it is agreeable to realize that in one and the same age translations were made of the *Art of Loving* and St. Bernard's Commentary on the Song. The author of a recent study of these translations has written, 'Is it not a thing to be admired that the *Sermons on the Song* belong in some way, by their translation, to religious literature of the romance tongue? From the end of the twelfth century, the public had access in everyday language to the masterpiece of sacred medieval eloquence. From the end of the twelfth century, French literature possesses pages of unequalled mystical elevation and uses as much art for singing the union between God and the soul as it did for celebrating the loves of Tristan or the adventures of Gawain. And just as for the wandering knight the middle of the day is the hour for adventure, so midday is the hour of contemplation in the full light of God, the end of the journey begun at the dawn of penance, which prefigures this other midday, the end of the journey begun at the dawn of Christ, the "eternal solstice" in the lasting presence of God. . . . Is it by chance that the same Bernard of Clairvaux, whose magnificent prose leads the reader at the close of the twelfth century towards the *eternal solstice*, becomes, a century later, the last of Dante's guides towards the love of God?'[88]

Finally, if in the variety of love literatures of the twelfth century there is any woman idealized, it is the bride of the Song: seen as such by Bernard and by monks, she announces and prepares Beatrice.

---

[1] E. Pellegrin, 'Quelques accessus au De amicitia de Cicéron', in *Hommage à André Boutemy*, Brussels, 1976, pp. 274–398.

[2] R. Gelsomino, 'S. Bernardo di Chiaravalle e il De amicitia di Cicerone', *Analecta monastica*, 5, Rome (*Studia Anselmiana*, 43), 1958, pp. 180–6.

[3] *De diligendo Deo*, 17.

[4] *De amicitia*, 100.

[5] Ibid. 30.

[6] *Sup. Cant.* 85. 5; *De dil. Deo*, 17.

[7] *Sup. Cant.* 83 and *passim*; *De dil. Deo*, 17.

[8] List of the Epistles in Gelsomino, loc. cit.; chronology of the Epistles in *S. Bernardi opera*, VII–VIII, Rome, 1974 and 1977.

[9] Gelsomino, loc. cit., p. 185.

[10] Ibid., pp. 185–6.

[11] S. Viarre, *La survie d'Ovide dans la littérature scientifique des XIIe et XIIIe siècles*, Poitiers, 1966.

[12] On all these points see, for example, P. Demats, *Fabula. Trois études de mythographie antique et médiévale*, Geneva, 1973, pp. 107-21; and P. Dronke, *Fabula: Explorations into the Uses of Myth in Medieval Platonism*, Leyden-Cologne, 1974.

[13] P. Dronke, 'Pseudo-Ovid, Facetus and the Arts of Love', *Mittellateinisches Jahrbuch*, 11 (1974), pp. 126-31; conclusion confirmed by K. Langosch, 'Der "Facetus, Moribus et vita" und seine Pseudo-Ovidiana', ibid., pp. 132-42; F. Schmitt-von Mühlenfels, *Pyramus und Thisbe. Rezeptionstypen eines ovidischen Stoffes in Literatur, Kunst und Musik*, Heidelberg, 1972.

[14] The most recent bibliography on this subject is in E. Pellegrin, loc. cit., pp. 274-5.

[15] Cf. *The Love of Learning and the Desire for God*, New York, 1977, p. 120.

[16] After Revilo P. Oliver, 'Interpolated lines in Ovid', in *Gesellschaft, Kultur, Literatur . . . Beiträge Luitpoldt Wallasch gewidmet*, Stuttgart, 1975, pp. 19-32.

[17] E. Pellegrin, 'Les Remedia amoris, texte scolaire médiéval', in *Bibliothèque de l'École des chartres*, 115 (1957), pp. 172-9.

[18] Cf. O. Schwencke, 'Zur Ovid-Rezeption im Mittelalter. Metamorphosen-Exempel in biblisch-exegetischem Volkschrifttum', *Zeitschrift für deutsche Philologie*, 89 (1970), pp. 336-46.

[19] Cf. P. Demats, op. cit., pp. 109-11; P. Ryan, 'The Influences of Seneca on William of Saint-Thierry', *Cîteaux*, 25 (1974), pp. 24-32.

[20] E. Pellegrin, 'Les Remedia amoris', loc. cit., p. 179.

[21] The most recent comprehensive study, with bibliography, is that of P. Ryan, 'The Influences of Seneca on William of Saint-Thierry', loc. cit.

[22] Ed. R. B. C. Huygens, *Accessus ad auctores*; Bernard of Utrecht, *Commentum in Theodulum*; Conrad of Hirsau, *Dialogus super auctores*, 1970, p. 51.

[23] P. Demats, op. cit., p. 116.

[24] *De natura et dignitate amoris*, I, *P.L.* 184. 381.

[25] For example, L. T. Topsfield, *Troubadours and Love*, Cambridge, 1975, pp. 104, 210, etc.; A. Roncaglia, *Civiltà cortese e civiltà borghese nel medioevo*, in *Concetti, storia, miti e immagini del medio evo*, a cura di Vittore Branca, Florence, 1973, pp. 277-8; and others.

[26] Already suggested in 1949 ('S. Bernard et Origène d'après un manuscrit de Madrid', *Rev. bénéd.* 59 (1949), p. 195, reprinted in *Recueil d'études*, II, p. 385), the fact that Bernard preached on the *De natura et dignitate amoris* has been confirmed on the basis of precise comparison of details by Stanislaus Ceglar, *William of Saint Thierry, The Chronology of his Life . . .*, Washington, D.C., 1971 (University Microfilms, Ann Arbor, Michigan), pp. 340-9.

[27] *Metam.* 1. 84-5.

[28] It comes up again, explicitly, attributed to 'a certain poet' whom everyone recognized, without it being necessary to name him, in *De div.* 100, *S. Bernardi opera*, VI. 1, Rome, 1970, p. 367.

[29] *Sent.* III. 125, *S. Bernardi opera*, VI. 2, Rome, 1972, p. 240.

[30] *In festiv. S. Martini*, 4, *S. Bernardi opera*, V, p. 402. 17.

[31] *Sup. Cant.* 24. 6, *S. Bernardi opera*, I, p. 157. 10. Such reminiscences must be added to the ten or so explicit quotations of Ovid which have been pointed out in Bernard's writings (*Bernard de Clairvaux*, Paris, 1953, pp. 551-2); even if we consider just these last quotations, Ovid was already the profane author most frequently quoted by St. Bernard.

[32] *Sup. Cant.* 71. 3, *S. Bernardi opera*, II, Rome, 1958, p. 216; cf. *Recueil d'études sur S. Bernard*, I, p. 292.

[33] This is a summary, given by R. Byrne, *Living the Contemplative Dimension in*

Everyday Life, Marquette, 1973, p. 17 (developed in pp. 18–20) (University Microfilms, Ann Arbor, Mich.), of E. W. Straus, 'Born to See, Bound to Behold: Reflections on the Functions of the Upright Posture in the Esthetic Attitude', in *The Philosophy of the Body*, edited by Stuart F. Spicker, Chicago, 1970, pp. 334–59.

³⁴ F. Gastaldelli, 'Amore e contemplazione in testi inediti claravallensi', *Salesianum*, 38 (1976), p. 46: 'Exceptiones de amore'. I thank the author of this article for having communicated to me a transcription of the quotations of the *Ars amandi* and the *Remedia* contained in this anthology.

³⁵ After John F. Benton, 'Clio and Venus: An Historical View of Medieval Love', in *The Meaning of Courtly Love*, ed. F. X. Newman, Albany, 1968, p. 31 and p. 41, n. 38.

³⁶ Cf. R. J. Cormier, *One Heart and One Mind: the Rebirth of Virgil's Hero in Medieval French Romance*, University of Mississippi, 1973, p. 53, with bibliography; H. Laurie, *Two Studies in Chrétien de Troyes*, Geneva, 1972, 'Index', pp. 219–21; 'A Note on the Composition of Marie's Guigemar', *Medium Aevum*, 44 (1975), p. 243, etc.

³⁷ Cf. R. Bossuat, art. 'Arts d'aimer (Les)', in *Dictionnaire des lettres françaises*, ed. G. Grente, 'Moyen âge', pp. 78–80.

³⁸ D. W. Robertson Jr., *A Preface to Chaucer, Studies in Medieval Perspectives*, Princeton, 1963, pp. 392–448. In the same sense by the same author, 'Two Poems from the Carmina Burana', *American Benedictine Review*, 27 (1976), pp. 36–59.

³⁹ R. Bossuat, art. 'André le Chapelain', in *Dictionnaire des lettres françaises*, 'Moyen âge', p. 55. The work, *De Amore*, is discussed below, pp. 115–19.

⁴⁰ In a study I am preparing on *The Language of Love*.

⁴¹ Ed. F. Branciforti, *Piramus et Tisbé. Introduzione, testo critico, traduzione e note*, Florence, 1959.

⁴² Cf. F. Schmitt-von Mühlenfels, quoted above, n. 13.

⁴³ S. Stronski, *Le troubadour Folquet de Marseille*, Cracow, 1910, p. 78*.

⁴⁴ *L'art d'amours. Traduction et commentaire de l'Ars amatoria d'Ovide*, by Bruno Roy, Leyden, 1974.

⁴⁵ Ibid., p. 45.

⁴⁶ For examples, see ibid., pp. 218, 219 and *passim*.

⁴⁷ p. 49.

⁴⁸ p. 114, ll. 1162–3.

⁴⁹ p. 115, l. 1173: S. of S. 5: 1, not identified as such in the edition.

⁵⁰ See below, Ch. IV.

⁵¹ pp. 114–15, 119.

⁵² p. 120, ll. 1316–18.

⁵³ p. 126, ll. 1437–9.

⁵⁴ pp. 133, 139.

⁵⁵ p. 117, ll. 1236–41.

⁵⁶ p. 144.

⁵⁷ For examples, see pp. 189, 190, etc.

⁵⁸ p. 145, ll. 1890–4.

⁵⁹ p. 148.

⁶⁰ p. 152.

⁶¹ pp. 156–7.

⁶² p. 159.

⁶³ 'Un témoin de l'antiféminisme au moyen âge', *Revue bénédictine*, 80 (1970), pp. 304–9.

⁶⁴ 'S. Pierre Damien et les femmes', *Studia monastica*, 15 (1973), pp. 43–55.

⁶⁵ 'S. Bernard et le féminin', in *Nouveau visage de Bernard de Clairvaux. Approches psycho-historiques*, Paris, 1976, pp. 127–54.

⁶⁶ See above, pp. 13–14.

[67] R. Javelet, *Image et ressemblance au XIIᵉ siècle, de Saint Anselme à Alain de Lille*, Paris, 1967, vol. I, p. 241.

[68] '"Ad ipsam sophiam Christum." Le témoignage monastique d'Abélard', *Revue d'ascétique et de mystique*, 46 (1970), pp. 161-82. On the liberty which Abelard took in modifying the Rule of St. Benedict when drafting a Rule for the Paraclete: R. Mohr, 'Der Gedankenaustausch Zwischen Heloisa und Abaelard über Eine Modifizierung der Regula Benedicti für Frauen', in *Regulae Benedicti Studia Annuarium Internationale*, ed. Bernard Jaspert and Eugene Manning O.C.R., vol. V (1976), published at Hildesheim, 1977, pp. 307-33.

[69] p. 167.

[70] p. 167.

[71] p. 175.

[72] Cf. *Études sur S. Bernard et le texte de ses écrits*, Rome, 1953, p. 137. St. Bernard, *In festo S. Michaelis*, 1. 3, *S. Bernardi opera*, V, p. 296. 1-5.

[73] p. 169.

[74] pp. 204-5.

[75] J. M. Déchanet, 'Le "naturam sequi" chez Guillaume de Saint-Thierry', in *Collectanea Ord. Cist. Ref.* 7 (1940), pp. 140-8.

[76] p. 206.

[77] p. 215.

[78] p. 219. 3444: Matt. 6: 24; and p. 220. 3453-5: 1 Cor. 12: 26.

[79] pp. 220-4.

[80] 'Huis et portes furent faiz pour y ceste chose', p. 214; 'Faire la chose', p. 223: this makes one think of the 'id' mentioned by certain modern psychologists.

[81] p. 219.

[82] E. Könsgen, *Epistolae duorum amantium. Briefe Abaelards und Heloïse?*, Leyden-Cologne, 1974.

[83] A few other texts may be added to those already identified in the edition.

[84] p. 16, *M* 25.

[85] p. 15, *M* 25; the expression *dilectionis debitum persolvere*, unidentified in the edition, has a precise meaning by the very fact that it is a reminiscence of St. Paul, 1 Cor. 7: 3: *Uxori vir debitum reddat . . . et uxor viro.*

[86] p. 6. 12 and p. 48. 85, the phrase beginning with *Si quicquid mundus* is inspired by both Cicero (cf. ibid., p. 6, n. 6) and S. of S. 8: 7.

[87] p. 14, l. 24.

[88] M. Zink, *La prédication en langue romane avant 1300*, Paris, 1976, p. 475.

V

Aggressiveness or Repression in St. Bernard and in his Monks

1. *Two levels of psyche in two forms of writings*

I SHALL attempt to develop here, with a minimum of psychological jargon, an intuition which dawned some thirty years ago with the discovery in manuscript form of some of Bernard's texts which had hitherto been unknown and the authenticity of which has since been established. These texts are to be found in Vol. VI, Part 2 of the recently published critical edition of Bernard's works. His major works, which have been edited at various times from the sixteenth century onwards, consist of treatises, letters, and sermons dictated to secretaries and intended for publication. They are of a markedly literary character, and were produced in a literary style. The other texts, consisting of *Sentences* and *Parables* may for the sake of convenience be called the 'minor works': not that they are unimportant, but because they are less formal in style and literary genre. Some of these minor works were known previously, but their authenticity had been questioned. Now, however, all of them, including some newly discovered texts, have been proved beyond doubt as being of St. Bernard. They are as it were the 'homely' or 'everyday' sermons he spoke familiarly to his monks in the language of everyday speech rather than in literary style. They have been preserved, not as edited by Bernard himself, but in redactions made by his listeners who later, and from memory, wrote down summaries—short sentences or more elaborate passages—of the addresses made to them by their abbot in the chapter house of the Abbey of Clairvaux.

The minor and major works reveal two different aspects of Bernard's personality, two different levels of his psyche expressed in two different modes of language. The major works reveal the level on which those thoughts arising from the deeper places of his psyche are given conscious and deliberately chosen expression. Here Bernard submits both his thought and expression to very strict social and literary controls governing matter and style in works intended for general circulation. Hence the significance of the many and sometimes extremely meticulous corrections he made in successive editions of his writings. Up till now these emendations have been studied from the point of view of literary excellence. But they also tell us something of Bernard's psychological make-up: the *emendatio* is not only a form of self-control but also a result of social controls.[1]

The minor works, on the other hand, reveal Bernard's spontaneous thought and unstudied manner of expressing himself. They throw light on his unconscious and also on his audience. They tell us something of the psychological character of these many, ordinary men who left no written works and whose psyche would remain unknown to us, were we not given a glimpse of it through what Bernard thought it necessary to tell them and the particular way—best suited to them—he chose to do so.

A similar case could be made with regard to another great spiritual writer, one who was of the generation prior to St. Bernard: St. Anselm of Canterbury, from whom we also have major dictated works—treatises, letters, meditations—and minor writings, namely the collection of *Sayings* (*Dicta*) and *Similitudines* redacted by his disciples.[2] For both St. Anselm and St. Bernard, but particularly St. Bernard, a very interesting study of the major and minor works can be made using skills from various disciplines: palaeography, codicology, historical criticism, sociology, literary analysis, psychology, theology, and spirituality.

Any such comparative study must be carried out on the basis of two sets of information: one concerns the literary genres, the other accrues from psychic patterns and images. Both allow us to pass from the analysis of conscious thought and expression to the discovery of the psyche at its deeper preconscious, subconscious, and unconscious levels. Neither one nor the other of these two sets of facts will allow of a facile approach to our study: literary forms and psychic patterns arise not only out of the individual consciousness, but are also dependent on traditional pre-biblical, biblical, post-biblical, and patristic elements. This tradition intervenes to modify and control the written expression of spontaneous experience. Despite all this, we may lawfully make some attempt to use modern psychological insights, and it will be interesting to do so in the two main fields of psychic experience: aggressiveness and love.

11. *Social aggressiveness as reflected in St. Bernard*

It is well known that a high degree of violence was characteristic of medieval life in all its aspects, including the religious aspect, and it manifested itself even in the realms of spirituality, piety, and popular devotion. Monks in the middle ages did not differ psychologically from their contemporaries, and they came from social milieux where violence was a commonplace and aggressive impulses were given free expression in a variety of conflicts and combats. A number of texts witness to the truth of this statement: for instance, the sacristy records of the Benedictine Abbey of Fleury from the tenth to the twelfth centuries,[3] the Decrees of the General Chapters of the Cistercian Order,[4] the Life of St. Stephen of Obazine.[5] But many other examples could be cited. The marvel is that monks drawn from a very violent society were not only less violent than the generality of people, but even, to some extent, succeeded in reconciling foes and bringing a degree of peace to the period.

The nobility most frequently found an outlet for aggression by fighting either in real wars of a rather localized nature—

from one neighbouring castle to another—or in mock combat and violent sports: tournaments, jousting, hunting of wild animals. Such a mode of life had previously been experienced by many, perhaps most, of the members of twelfth-century Cistercian communities which were not recruited from child oblates but from youths and young adults educated to a life of arms and knightly chivalry. Some were snatched from the very heat of battle for service of Christ in Cistercian life. Such had been the case with Bernard's brothers and kinsmen: when he wanted to convert them to the monastic life, he went to a castle where a battle was in progress and in which one of them was wounded.[6] Later on, he worked the 'beer miracle', in which the blessing called down on the beer became a grace of conversion for a group of noble youths visiting Clairvaux and who shortly after all returned to the monastery to become novices.

It is related that a troop of noble soldiers—*nobilium cohors militum*—turned off the route on which they were journeying in order to visit Clairvaux and see its holy abbot. The holy season of Lent was approaching and almost all these young men, who were dedicated to secular knighthood, went about from one jousting ground to another to take part in tournaments. Bernard asked them to lay down their arms during the few days before Lent began, but they obstinately refused to heed his advice. So he summoned one of the brethren to bring some beer, which he blessed. They drank and rode off, but soon returned to Clairvaux to enlist in the spiritual knighthood. Some of them are still warring for God—*adhuc militant Deo*—while others now reign with him.[7]

Thus their monastic life and even their eternal life is presented as a continuation of their secular *militia*.

It is known that many of the monks at Clairvaux at the time of Bernard had been knights, schooled in arms and versed in the romances of chivalry and courtly literature. But whatever the social strata from which the monks were drawn, they were children of their age and so, to a greater or lesser extent, they were familiar with, and influenced by, the songs and stories of the day. They were consequently open to the excitement and challenge of the romances in which military adventures occupied such a large place; linked as they so often were with a love motif. For example, in Chrétien de Troyes and throughout the Arthurian cycle, love is proved by feat of arms and won by combat for the lady's favour. Such literary expression of romantic love came more naturally to the men of this age, who found it easier to describe at length armed contests and knightly tournaments than to catch in words the subtleties of sentiment or the nuances of love-making. We can readily understand, however, the widespread interest in that particular type of literature, and it is highlighted by an incident which may have taken place towards the end of the twelfth century and which is related by Caesarius of Heisterbach, who tells of a ruse devised by a Cistercian abbot to recapture his monks' wandering attention during his sermon: an instance of the clear recognition and acceptance by the abbot of a continuing interest in romance as being part of the psychological baggage carried by medieval monks:

On a certain solemnity, Gevardus, predecessor of the present abbot, was giving us a talk in the Chapter. He noticed that some, especially among the conversi, had gone to sleep; a few were even snoring. So he raised his voice: 'Listen, my brothers,' he said, 'I have something new and important to tell you. There was a King called Arthur.' There his story ended, but he went on to say: 'My brothers, this is no light matter; you went to sleep when I spoke of God—but as soon as I introduced a diverting theme you pricked up your ears, woke up, and began to listen.' I was present at that sermon. The devil tempts by sleep spiritual and worldly people alike.[8]

In this text it is interesting to note that special mention is made of the *conversi*. These did not come from among the student or clerical classes in the schools, but mainly from the knights, burghers, and peasantry. Whatever may have been their origins, most monks continued to have an interest in the literature of chivalry, which became more and more a literature of courtly love, and furthermore they had personal memories of past adventures as knights-at-arms. Thus it is no matter for astonishment that the aggressive images conveyed by such

literature should be a mine of association and potential motivation. This is possibly why St. Bernard at the beginning of his
long and splendid exposition of the Song of Songs insistently
compares monastic life and asceticism to military service, and
the community to a *militia* doing battle for the king.[9] We must
not forget, however, that this was a traditional theme contained
in biblical, patristic, and early monastic sources. Thus the fact
that St. Bernard used it does not necessarily presuppose dependence on the thought patterns underlying knightly romances, nor
does it imply a reflection of the mental categories of feudal times.
Occasionally, as for example in his first letter to his cousin
Robert, Bernard very evidently uses court language.[10] But this
is not frequent in his major works, with the exception of the
treatise *In Praise of the New Militia: to the Knights of the
Temple.*[11]

These more important writings also show that Bernard had a
very precise and elaborate doctrine of war, of protocol for waging
it in a just cause and with right motives. In this rather circum-
scribed area of his thought, he propounds a theology of re-
strained violence which is the outcome of very deliberate
reflection and meditation. These ideas of his have been studied
in detail elsewhere, however.[12]

Let us now examine Bernard's spontaneous reaction to
chivalry and knighthood as revealed by his minor works. It is
convenient for this study to examine first the *Parables*, even
though we shall have to return to them later when speaking of
Bernard's use of the language of love. These texts are more or
less similar to short stories, some of which may be as many as ten
pages in length. A number of them have been preserved in
manuscripts in different redactions. This is sure proof that
St. Bernard, who did not himself dictate and publish them, was
fond of developing the same theme on various occasions. There
are eight *Parables* in all. Six of them, and one of the *Sentences*
(III. 51), take the form of romances in which the story of God's
great love for mankind is unfolded, God so loving man as to
unite himself to human nature by the incarnation of his Son,

and this despite man's sinfulness and infidelity, and after long deliberations between the divine attributes, personified as the 'daughters' of God. In each of the six Bernard uses images and metaphors from feudal life generally and from the institution of chivalry in particular. So both the dramatis personae and the stage settings are direct borrowings from the contemporary society: there is a king, a queen, a royal family, a court, a palace, and a council of princes; then there is an army, a fortress, a camp, a siege, a beleagured city, assaulted with the help of machines of war. Even Pharaoh and his soldiers are described as medieval warriors, with the helmet and armour in which they are depicted in paintings and sculptures, in the frescoes, and on the capitals of the day. We may easily imagine the interest that the monks, as ex-knights, gave to such parables: perhaps there was a certain tension too, as nostalgia alternated with whimsical joy and delighted amusement at finding again in spiritual theology, in the Bible, and even in God himself, qualities and attributes explicable in terms of symbols and images from a way of life still so fresh in their memories.

These symbols from life at court and in the field of war are to be found in the first of the *Parables*. The second, *About a War Between Two Kings*, gives an account of a long-drawn-out struggle between the two. In it we find all the adventures commonly associated with protracted hostilities: there are the preparations, the planning of the campaign, attacks, truces, ambushes, engagements between lines of horsemen, each with his attendant armour-bearer; then the battle is engaged and all seems total confusion; but finally the enemy forces are put to headlong flight. Then the gates of the relieved city are flung wide and the victor king enters in triumph.

The same themes and images, with slight variations, are further developed in Parables III, IV, V, and VI. Quite evidently such literary devices, coloured by memories and associations from former days, never failed to evoke a response in Bernard's audience. By means of them the aggressive impulses which the monks had retained from their previous life were

safely discharged and healthily sublimated in a spiritual engage-
ment: doing battle and winning glory for the sake of divine love
and the Divine Lover.

It is also easy to understand why similar stories occur in the
teaching of St. Anselm[13] and in Galland of Régny, a contemporary and admirer of St. Bernard.[14] But in the abbot of Clairvaux,
all the vivacity of his imagination, all his wealth of fantasy and
gift of poetry combined with the intensity of his temperament to
give these little romances an exceptional beauty and provocative
power. Every hearer identified himself with the hero of the
romance. He felt in himself the same desire to do battle with
the enemy; he knew from experience the same sense of strength
and skill as the knight-at-arms; and at the same time he
rejoiced to know that his cause was noble and just, his motives
pure.

In the *Sentences* we find a theme to which Bernard returned
time and time again in his exegesis of biblical texts. It is symbolized by the horses and chariots of Pharaoh's army.[15] They are
mentioned in the Song of Songs, and the Book of Exodus tells
how they were vanquished by the troops of Moses. Bernard likes
to dwell on the chariots and their riders in detail, attributing to
each detail a certain symbolism: the chariots themselves, their
wheels, the horses and their harness, their saddles, their bridles
and bits, and lastly the horsemen, with all their accoutrement
from helmet down to spurs. Such a flood of fantasy might seem
to us undisciplined, excessive, and in bad taste for an author. But
Bernard in his major works did not write in such a style. In fact,
there is only one instance of unbridled symbolism in a major
work—the thirty-ninth Sermon on the Song of Songs. And there
Bernard did know where to draw the rein. In works meant for
publication he did not elaborate his thought by adding symbolic
detail to symbolic detail as he did when in a playful mood and
among his brethren. Rather, on more formal occasions, by
deft use of symbols he evoked a chain of associations and
suggested a train of thought to be developed imaginatively by
his listeners.

Here again it is easy to understand why this symbolism had such telling effects on the monks, making them feel at home, as it were, in the Kingdom. We find in the *Sentences* twenty or so other instances when St. Bernard speaks with greater or less detail of monks as a *militia* and of the monastic life in terms of spiritual combat. These texts may be grouped into two categories: those which speak of battle and those which deal with armament. Among the texts of the first class it is worthwhile drawing attention to a word which is most significant for a study of Bernard's use of language in his domestic sermons.

When speaking of King Solomon as a prefiguring of Christ, Bernard says of the latter: 'Ipse est enim qui pacificavit illam inexorabilem guerram inter homines et angelos' (*Sent.* III. 87).[16] Elsewhere too, in the first version of one of his sermons, Bernard had used at first *guerra*, sometimes written in manuscripts as *werra*, and corresponding with the French word, *guerre*, and the English, *war*. Later, when editing the text, he realized that the word *guerra* was out of keeping with a correct, classical Latin vocabulary, and he then substituted the word *bellum*.[17] This change, and others of a like kind, indicate that Bernard's spontaneous thought and expression were not in Latin. When thinking to himself, when addressing his ordinary, familiar audience, the vernacular, not Latin, came more readily to Bernard's mind and lips: and it was the vernacular of the French Romance of his native Burgundy and of Southern Champagne, in which Clairvaux was situated. It was only when preparing texts for general publication that he expressed himself in Latin, and even then, at times, he wrote a first draft containing elements of spontaneous Latin having its roots in his vernacular speech.

What is here said of Bernard's vernacular expression can also be said of what might be called his vernacular thought processes. This is evident if we consider how he thinks of war. Sometimes he writes simply of an attack *à main armée*, by main force of strong right arms. But he continues in correct Latin: ... *iumentumque carnis in his duobus aculeis agitatur* (II. 1), to describe how the body reels beneath the blows just as an animal shies when stung in two places at once. At other times, however, his thought is more complex and couched in the Latin military vocabulary. For we must not forget that these short sentences are mere summaries of longer conferences wherein his themes were more fully developed. In fact, in the sentence following the one just quoted, we find the verb 'to serve as a soldier' (*militare*) used five times, along with other words from the vocabulary of war: to attack (*oppugnare*), young recruits (*tirones*), captivity (*captivitas*), etc. This martial vocabulary of combat and struggle evokes an association of Jacob struggling against Esau, against God, with Laban, and with the angel—his opponents all serving as symbols of the adversaries with whom Bernard's hearers (and we also) have to do battle in the spiritual life (III. 39). A further biblical model is provided by David, killing Goliath with his own sword and serving Bernard's didactic purpose of showing how his monks must slay vainglory (III. 32b). At other times Bernard pictures man as a fortress besieged on every side. He then enumerates all the parts of the citadel and gives every detail of the conduct of the siege: there is a castle (*castellum*), a wall (*murus*), an outer wall (*ante murale*), a watch-tower (*turris*), and weapons (*arma*); then Bernard makes direct application of all this to the spiritual combat, at times indulging in even more elaborate detail than he does in this case. 'A triple line of fortification protects the soul: It is fenced round by the assiduous practice of discretion; it finds a strong citadel in the intercession of the saints; and it is completely enclosed in the divine protection which is proof against all the onslaughts of the evil one.'

We are also told of the four ways in which the soul can be ensnared: *quatuor sunt quibus anima captivatur* (II. 155). And right at the very beginning of the first series of these sentences is one which, so to speak, sets the tone for all the rest. It is a story, given in some detail, of a king's son captured in war. We are told of the battle in which he is taken prisoner; of the messenger sent secretly and making his way through the enemy lines undetected to be received by the king under cover of darkness in the very early morning. Having made all possible speed, the messenger reaches the royal court, gains entry to the king's presence and successfully negotiates the dispatch of an army to free the king's son and his fellow captives. Thus, because of the king's love for his son and for his people, all ends happily. But it should be noted that, throughout the whole tale, war and violence feature more prominently than peace and charity.

In yet another group of sentences, Bernard seems to take delight in speaking of those weapons formerly carried and wielded by many of his hearers. Sometimes he treats of them in general terms, contrasting the weapons of virtue with those brandished by evil: *Arma virtutis, quibus arma nequitiae expugnantur*; or, in yet another place, he names particular weapons, or by the energy of his expression suggests strong aggressive force: *expellit, contra . . . contra . . .* (II. 26); it is driven forth . . . against . . . against. . . .

And he speaks too of the arrow, the most common weapon in the middle ages. Always there is a sheaf of arrows, three being the minimum (II. 13). With them the Lord wounds his adversary before closing in for hand-to-hand combat: *Dominus habet proprias sagittas, quibus hostes vulnerat, et in brachio virtutis expugnat. Sunt autem tres sagittae, quibus hostes sauciantur. . . .* The rest of the sentence is concerned with the auxiliary forces of the enemy, the *satellites*, and with a description of the fortifications with which he is hedged round on every side: *se undique circumsaeptum* (II. 12). Four weapons are described with great exactitude in II. 152; and elsewhere he speaks of the shield (*scutum*), the breastplate (*thorax*), and the lance (*lancea*) (III. 38). And on one occasion, we seem to be present when a knight is being clad in full armour:

Unity is served by three weapons: patience, humility, and charity. With these the soldier of Christ should be armed. He should bear the shield of patience as a defence against all adversity. The corslet of humility should be as a guard on his heart, and in his hand charity should be a weapon of offence in the warfare of the Lord, since, as the Apostle says, appeal to the Lord should be made for all undertakings and in love's name all should be carried through. And on his head, protecting it as the seat of thought, should rest the helmet of salvation. God's word should be the sword in his hand and good desires the steed upon which he is mounted.

We can readily imagine Bernard explaining the symbolism of the various items of the monastic habit as he conferred it piece by piece at the clothing or profession of a former knight; and doing so in terms of the weapons and insignia with which he had been invested as a knight, but transposing their meaning in the light of a court and service higher than that which gave significance to the worldly ceremony.

Now, has it been worth our while to linger so long on these minor texts, to which, until the present time, so little attention has been paid? I think it has. Because these texts not only tell us something of Bernard's pedagogical method when training his monks, but also give us a glimpse of his and their psyches. Let us notice at once that he grounds his formation on an element in his and their past experience—the presence in them of an aggressive impulse to be given a needed outlet in action. He does not deny the existence of this need; he does not suppress it. He faces up to the facts; he admits that his monks, in common with himself, know the appeal of a call to arms; are under the necessity of releasing the aggressiveness within. So he gives the impulse new direction and a new meaning by enlisting it in the service of Christ, by engaging it in the spiritual combat of a life according to monastic values.

Bernard made symbolic reference to aggression frequently enough and clearly enough to awaken in the psyche of his hearers memories of personal acts of violence, and to arouse pleasurable images or desires, the satisfaction of which, by actual force of arms, they had freely renounced. But those memories and impulses remained alive in their unconscious ever ready to surface to conscious level, even if only in disguise. This Bernard realized, it seems. Much better to face these basic human impulses at the conscious, voluntary level in order to control them, than to strive to continuously repress them.

Bernard used two ruses to sublimate the dynamics of aggression in his monks. In the first place he readily and frequently had recourse to the Bible, narrating in its own words the conflicts and struggles endured by biblical characters. The use of sacred language had the effect of expelling, as it were, the evil conveyed by the literal sense, with the result that both words and realities were raised to the spiritual plane of the history of salvation. In this way the abbot helped his monks to realize that by their day-to-day combat in monastic ascesis they were made part of the divine plan for mankind. Secondly, Bernard had a way of putting each symbol of aggression in juxtaposition to the spiritual realities which are the components of the peace resulting from the Christian combat: such combat vanquishes evil and establishes the soul in peace. We have, for example, battle put in opposition to charity (I. 7); weapons (the symbol of division) are in contrast to unity (I. 1); struggle is the condition for attaining to the beatitudes (II. 2); arrows are the defence of sweetness, love, desire for God (II. 13); weapons are used to protect sanctity (II. 26); divine protection is a fortress (II. 105); and an array of virtues is depicted as a suit of armour (II. 152).

We could possibly epitomize St. Bernard's pedagogy in the formula, 'To instil inner peace instruct in inner warfare'. Using biblical terminology and playing on his monks' past experience, this was precisely the method he used to sublimate their aggressive forces, instructing them how to wield the arms of spiritual warfare and interiorize the values of the way of peace in which they had chosen to walk. As in his major works, so in his everyday sermons at Clairvaux, Bernard could have left aside these martial symbols and similes, but, astute psychologist that he was, he preferred to adapt himself to the psyche of those monks whose minds were stamped with knightly images from past experiences or reading and in whom—in contradistinction to the wide anonymous public of his major treatises—still burned the fires of ardent chivalry. He transformed his monastic recruits into soldiers of peace—*bellatores pacifici*[18]—and thus trained, in hundreds of monasteries, an immense peace corps.

III. *Transformation of a desire for human love into a desire for
union with God*

In 1124 or 1125 St. Bernard wrote of love in Letter 11,[19] and
from then onward love was a recurrent theme in all his writings
up to the very last days of his life, when he left unfinished his
long commentary on the Song of Songs, begun in 1135.[20] The
treatise *On the Necessity of Loving God*[21] was redacted between
1126 and 1141. These are all major works and reveal, quite
obviously, both his theology and his psychology of love. However, in some of the minor works, the *Parables* for example,
Bernard's teaching and experience are conveyed in a literary
genre similar in many ways to the love literature of his own times
and social background.

Hence the importance of considering the immediate environment in which Bernard moved and had his being. Clairvaux, it
must be remembered, was in the vicinity of Troyes, seat of the
Counts of Champagne. The court there was a renowned centre
of chivalry and courtly literature, as John F. Benton has pointed.
Moreover, this town of Troyes will ever remain associated with
the great troubadour Chrétien and his cycle of love romances,
the first to be written in that area. It is an interesting coincidence,
too, that it was in Champagne that Abelard founded the
monastery of the Paraclete for Héloïse.[22]

It is quite natural that in such an environment the language of
chivalry and the court, and the love literature which flowed from
them should be familiar to all. It was part of the very air of the
province, breathed in and savoured by nobles in their castles,
burghers in the town, peasants on the farms, and even by a
number of clerics who are known to have written some of the
troubadour songs. The remarkable thing about these romances is
that they sang not so much of love of man for woman—though
love-making is to some extent present in them—as of tournaments, jousts, and all kinds of military adventures. They very
frequently tell of the winning of a beloved lady's hand by greatly
arduous feats of knightly valour or of a knight proving his love

for his lady by marvellous deeds of courage. These feats are
recounted in the great narrative cycles of the time, such as the
Legend of the Holy Grail and other derivatives from the
Arthurian legend, which, as Caesarius of Heisterbach has shown,
so deeply influenced the psyche of many twelfth-century monks.

We are now in a position to ask whether Bernard's writings
reflect the literature and language of love so common in his
neighbourhood. First, however, we must ask, outright, whether
it was fitting for a monk and an abbot to talk to his community
of human love. This question is of importance because recently
a writer has published a new interpretation of Bernard in which
it is declared categorically that Bernard from adolescence onwards had been obsessed by his sexuality; that he had harshly
repressed his sexual urges and continued throughout life to do
so. In the light of this alleged repression, this violent over-
reaction, everything in Bernard's life is interpreted. His works
and writings, his monastic and church reforms, his politics, his
part in the Crusades, his controversy with Abelard, his commentary on the Song of Songs—all are declared to be the outcome
of sexual repression.[23]

Even a hasty reading of the primary sources—Bernard's own
works—and some knowledge of the secondary ones—works
written about him—would have saved this author from such a
fanciful and simplistic interpretation of the complexity of
Bernard's personality. It has not been difficult to rebut the
charges and to establish the fact that nothing in the historical
evidence as we have it supports this interpretation. This study,
as so often is the case with hagiography, tells more about the
author than about his subject, as we shall see later.

In such matters we must be careful not to project on to a less
erotically preoccupied society the artificially stimulated and
commercially exploited eroticism of our own sex-ridden age.
But neither should we be afraid to face the facts and take the
texts as Bernard wrote them.

In the first place we find that Bernard does not hesitate to make
use of strong sexual imagery, which writers, secular and religious,

in more sexually self-conscious periods, would not have dared to use, even though most of the images used by Bernard are biblical in origin. In another place I have given some examples of these as they occur in the *Sentences*;[24] here let it suffice to mention the very precise description of circumcision (I. 14) and of the stimulation of sexual impulses (II. 97).

What has Bernard to say of love? As far as the emotions and the affective attitudes or the heightened activity of a man and woman in love are concerned, he adds little to what was already to be found in the Song of Songs. But he comments on all the elements of this relationship with a disarming frankness and freedom which perhaps became a source of scandalized surprise to the pious in the later periods of history. Hence a very interesting field of study is to be found in the consideration of Bernard's reaction to the 'feminine'.[25] However, love between the sexes is but one expression of Christian love. There is also the love of charity and it is that which we find overflowing from the works of the abbot of Clairvaux. The purity and the orthodoxy of faith is a form of such love, and Bernard is concerned that this should be found in his monks, which explains, perhaps, that in the *Sentences* he mentions heresy a dozen or so times as against the rare use of the word elsewhere.[26] That William of Saint-Thierry was preoccupied with Abelard as a threat to orthodoxy is well known. But we have no indication that Bernard was unduly worried about Abelard. It was only during 1139–1140, when he was officially constituted defender of the Church's teaching, that he called him a heretic.[27] On the other hand, the more popular heresies of the neo-Manichaeans—the so-called 'cathars'—which were infiltrating everywhere caused him no little anxiety. These teachings held little attraction for those who read Bernard's major works, but for his monks, more often schooled in chivalry than in theology, they were a real danger. Thus the abbot was obliged to point out their falsity and to warn his monks against them.

In the minor works we find several passages in which Bernard makes very precise use of the language of human love to develop his theme of love between Christ and the Church. One of the *Sentences* (III. 51) takes its inspiration from that charming biblical novel, the Book of Ruth: just as Boaz loves Ruth, so Christ loves his Church; but similarly, just as Ruth had to be freed and raised to a higher plane, namely that of Boaz, so the Church had to be liberated to attain union with her Lord. In this instance Bernard uses language taken both from the Book of Ruth and the Song of Songs, to give us a beautiful transformation of a human love story into a profoundly Christological and ecclesiological exposition of the love of Christ for the Church.

But more frequently he used a literary expression in which the vocabulary of human love is mixed with that of chivalry and war. In another of the *Sentences* (III. 122), Bernard makes his commentary on the nuptial symbols of the Song of Songs, in the form of a dramatic account of a young girl, betrothed to a prince, who had been taken captive and sold as a slave in Egypt. The prince makes war to save her. He is victorious, vanquishes her captors, but having no desire to be, as it were, her captor in his turn, wishes her to be completely free in giving herself to him, 'just as the law of marriage requires'. Bernard's use of biblical quotations makes of the story a recapitulation of salvation history; in symbol, the rescued girl is the Daughter of Zion; the physical union so intimately described by Bernard is an image of the marriage of God with his people. Then, as is the case, too, in salvation history, husband and wife are separated; in his absence she is recaptured, only to be freed once more by him, these further adventures leading to final and definitive union between the two.

The same kind of story is found as a first redaction—'oral style'—of the *Fourth Sermon for the Feast of the Annunciation* and in the *Parables*: the beloved is won by the same chivalrous adventures and force of arms; again there is an unabashed description of human love-making: again biblical language is used for the marriage-bed and to describe the lover's kiss and embrace. These little romances always end in a happy marriage, ever, for Bernard, the symbol of the intimate union of the Church with her King, as well as of the union of the individual soul with her Lord in the Church and monastic life.

Bernard skilfully uses these stories with their images of war and captivity, especially captivity in Egypt, to make his hearers realize what it is to be a sinner, in the bonds of sin, far from one's homeland. And further, in these commentaries, he uses the biblical symbol of liberation, again especially from Egypt, to bring his monks to an understanding of what it is to be a forgiven sinner, full of joy, peace, and love as he returns to his own land. Bernard's approach was realistic for all its poetry and imagery, for it must not be forgotten how real was captivity far from home for people of his times and especially for those of the monk's social class: captivity by the Saracens was an experience common enough for knights in the twelfth century.

Once again, we see St. Bernard effecting a sublimation of a basic human impulse, that of love. His method in this instance is very similar to that we have seen him adopt with regard to aggression: he uses a genuine language of human love made familiar to his monks through courtly literature, if by no other means. But by using biblical language to express the human impulses and emotions he transports human love to a higher plane, where the figures in the human drama become transformed into symbols of God and his beloved people, or of the human soul beloved by God and with whom the monks could readily identify. By the words of the inspired texts the emotions of the hearers are purified of their carnal elements, and the strong emotive power channelled into motivation for service of Christ in love. This frequent, even continuous, teaching, with biblical imagery transposing human love to a spiritual level, lifting it from the infraconscious and spontaneous areas of the psyche to that of the conscious and deliberate choice of options, ensured an ongoing sublimation of the monk's spontaneous emotional energies and enabled them to grow and develop, to pass over, as it were, to a plane of faith reality which their abbot desired them to reach. The texts which have been put forward confirm the difference noticed above between the psychology of the new monasticism and that of the old. At Clairvaux and in its foundations, many monks shared in the work of writing and copying, preserving, reading, and meditating on the manuscripts of St. Bernard. There are dozens of manuscripts[28] preserved; they seem to have been living texts, constantly adapted, abridged, developed, and modified according to the needs of those who heard them or read them; they were a part of their lives. For the traditional monasticism, we have at our disposal a series of relevant texts from the same literary genre: these are the *Dicta* of St. Anselm, probably written down before 1109, and the *Similitudines*, short stories, sentences, parables, collected about 1130.[29] These two collections show how St. Anselm spoke to the monks of Bec. The theme of the *militia* is there; the comparison of a monk with a knight is evoked by an encampment (*castra*), a squadron of troops, a knight's armour.[30] But these images occupy incomparably less space than in the writings of Bernard. Metaphors borrowed from fornication, adultery, married union, a husband (never a wife, note) are rare and not very prominent.[31] No story of love is told, and in more than 300 pages of text I have found only two quotations from the Song of Songs.[32] Obviously, St. Anselm was speaking to former children of the cloister, and he speaks their language, while St. Bernard had in front of him an audience of converted young knights and he uses language belonging to their former life in order to make them understand the meaning of their new way of life.

Bernard's complete pedagogy was aimed at recognizing and accepting the whole dimension of the psyche: by means of parables and symbols taken from current literature and contemporary experience he attempted to bring the more or less hidden impulses, motives, and memories of the infraconscious into the light, to effect a recognition and acceptance by the monks of their spontaneous selves and then, by a process of sublimation and by the word of Scripture addressed to them, to raise them consciously to the supraconscious levels of the psyche where basic human needs become freely chosen options, accepted values, and a fertile field for religious experience. Is such sure psychological guidance a proof that Bernard had first trodden that way himself? Possibly.

IV. *Conclusion. The oneness of the two psychic levels in
St. Bernard*

We have seen the purpose of St. Bernard's teaching and the ideal to which it was orientated. But exactly how successful was his method, for himself in the first instance, and then for his monks? Did they, on the whole, come to that psychological 'passover' which leads from bondage to spontaneous impulses to freedom as fully integrated personalities? For Bernard himself there is ample evidence, but a wider study would possibly be needed in the case of his monks. It must be admitted, however, that the use of such methods, with the frank expression of the language of aggression and sexual love, has its peculiar risks. We may wonder whether Bernard's pedagogy was always free from such risks and from all ambiguity. Though there is no absolute answer to such a query, one thing is certain: Bernard was a unified personality. In addition to an ardent temperament and great strength of emotion, he possessed that quality of joyousness which is recognized as the hallmark of an integrated person. And he possessed it to a remarkable degree, and by conscious options with regard to this dimension of his psychic life. His published works show an explicit doctrine of joy, of human happiness and what he called 'joyous devotion', *iucunda devotio*.[33] He had, too, a sense of humour as is abundantly clear in these same works.[34] But humour and happiness are even more in evidence in his minor works and they undoubtedly account for much of the attraction which he held for other people. The *Sentences*, in particular, have much that is humorous, witty, even jocose; consequently they were full of appeal for his hearers: the lessons he strove to teach were driven home with pleasantry and charm as well as real wisdom and love for the monks themselves. Such teaching could not fail to be effective; but this aspect of Bernard has been treated elsewhere.

It would be pointless to ask who is the real Bernard—the Bernard of the great theological works with their carefully chosen and developed themes and the polished style, or Bernard the Father Abbot, at home with his monks, men of his own race and class to a great extent, informally teaching them, sharing his spiritual adventures with them as gaily as formerly they had shared adventures in field or court. Here we have not two Bernards but one, a unified, integrated person who had brought his spontaneous impulses into the full freedom of service of God through love. His writings reveal the two ways in which he expressed his own basic human needs and more absolute values. In the minor works we find more spontaneity because Bernard was relating to a more familiar, affectionate, personal environment. In the major works there is a different orchestration of needs and environment, but it is the same man who reveals himself to us, playing a more self-controlled and more socially controlled concerto in a different key.

In the treatise *On the Necessity of Loving God*, Bernard proves that divine love integrates and assumes all human manifestations of love which are in harmony with the divinely established order of values, be it married love or celibate love. It is not the moment to analyse this treatise from that point of view. The limited purpose of this chapter has been to illustrate, in the light of some examples, the interaction between Bernard's human needs and his environment, and to show how he achieved an integration and psychic unity, happily expressed in symbolic language realistically appropriate to both.

We can say that Bernard's psyche was the psyche of an integrated personality constantly in touch with his times and its people. Yet, too, he transcended his age and his milieu, reconciling their conflicting human and divine aspirations through his teaching. This gave hidden and spiritual significance to the external social manifestation not only of man's compulsions to aggressiveness and love, but also of the conflict between his spontaneous self-centredness and a Christ-centred desire for God. St. Bernard kept his finger on the pulse of his age and was therefore in real communion with it. This allowed him to express its deepest aspirations and conflicts in language movingly human yet symbolically divine. His words lifted men's hearts to long for God, to hunger for his compassionate and liberating love. Was it any wonder that he should, as a person, have had such great and ennobling influence not only on his monastic foundations but also on his own immediate surroundings and on secular society as a whole? Michel Zink has clearly demonstrated how the literature of chivalry and the court received a decisive impulse from the writings of Bernard of Clairvaux. According to his wishes, the *Sentences*, redacted by monks for monks, had but a limited monastic circulation. But a wider reading public was interested in two of the Parables, I and IV, which because of their kinship with courtly literature had great appeal for general readers when recast as one long story published in French. The first translator of the *Sermons on the Song of Songs* adapted them, modified them to make them suitable for courtly readers.[35] The translation had something of the freshness, the spontaneity, and boyish charm of the abbot's everyday talks to his monks at Clairvaux, those ex-knights who had laid down their arms and enlisted in the new *militia*, as champions in a new Kingdom, not of this world, and conquerors of a new love.

[1] These 'author's corrections' are studied from the literary point of view in *Recueil d'études sur S. Bernard*, 4 vols., Rome, 1962-77.

[2] *S. Anselmi Cantuariensis Archiepiscopi Opera Omnia*, ed. F. S. Schmitt, 6 vols., Seckau-Edinburgh, 1938-61; *Memorials of St. Anselm*, ed. R. W. Southern and F. S. Schmitt, London, 1969.

[3] 'Violence and Devotion to St. Benedict', *Downside Review*, 88 (1970), pp. 344-60.

[4] A. Dimier, 'Violences, rixes et homicides chez les Cisterciens', *Revue des sciences religieuses*, 46 (1972), pp. 38-57.

[5] 'Modern Psychology and the Interpretation of Medieval Texts', *Speculum*, 48 (1973), pp. 479-81.

[6] William of Saint-Thierry, *S. Bernardi Vita Prima*, I. 10-12, *P.L.* 185. 232-4.

[7] Ibid. 55, 257.

[8] *Caesarii Heisterbacensis Dialogus Miraculorum*, ed. J. Strange, Cologne, 1851, Distinctio 4, cap. 36, p. 105.

[9] *S. Bernardi opera*, I, pp. 3-4.

[10] *S. Bernardi opera*, VII, pp. 10-11; other instances are Epistles 2, 3, in VII, p. 14, and *Apologia*, 22, in III, p. 99.

¹¹ *S. Bernardi opera*, III, pp. 213-39.

¹² 'L'attitude spirituelle de S. Bernard devant la guerre', *Collectanea Cisterciensia*, 36 (1974), pp. 195-227; 'Pour l'histoire de l'encyclique de S. Bernard sur la croisade', in *Mélanges E. R. Labande, Études de civilisation médiévale (Xᵉ-XIIᵉ siècles)*, Poitiers, 1974, pp. 479-90; B. Flood, 'St. Bernard's View of Crusade', *Australasian Catholic Record*, 47 (1970), pp. 130-8.

¹³ *Memorials of St. Anselm* (see n. 2), pp. 97-102.

¹⁴ 'Les paraboles de Galland de Régny', *Analecta Monastica Studia Anselmiana*, 20, Rome, 1948, I, p. 176, n. 21, and pp. 178-80.

¹⁵ *S. Bernardi opera*, II, pp. 21-3. On this symbolism of the chariots see *Recueil d'études sur S. Bernard*, III, pp. 151-8.

¹⁶ In the following pages, in similar references, the abbreviation *Sent.* stands for *Sententiae*, the first number is that of one of the three series of Sentences, the second number is that of the Sentence in that series.

¹⁷ *Recueil d'études sur S. Bernard*, III, pp. 169 and 317.

¹⁸ Applied by Bernard to the Premonstratensians in his Letter 355, *S. Bernardi opera*, VIII, p. 299.

¹⁹ *S. Bernardi opera*, VII, pp. 52-60.

²⁰ On this chronology see *Recueil d'études sur S. Bernard*, I, pp. 221-43.

²¹ *S. Bernardi opera*, III, pp. 52-60.

²² See below, Ch. VI.

²³ William E. Phipps, art. cit. Cf. 'Agressivité et répression chez Bernard de Clairvaux', *Revue d'histoire de la spiritualité*, 52 (1976), pp. 155-72.

²⁴ Introduction to the *Sentences*, in *Opere di S. Bernardo*, Milan, 1978, forthcoming.

²⁵ *Nouveau visage de Bernard de Clairvaux*, Paris, 1976, Ch. 6: 'S. Bernard et le féminin', pp. 127-54.

²⁶ 'L'hérésie d'après les écrits de S. Bernard' in *The Concept of Heresy in the Middle Ages*, Louvain and The Hague, 1976, pp. 12-26.

²⁷ 'Pour un portrait spirituel de Guillaume de Saint-Thierry', forthcoming in the proceedings of the Conference on the History of the Abbey of Saint-Thierry, Reims, October 1976.

²⁸ One hundred and three manuscripts of the *Parables* are listed in H. Rochais, 'Enquête sur les sermons divers et les sentences de S. Bernard', *Analecta Sacri Ordinis Cisterciensis*, 18 (1963), fasc. 3-4, pp. 31-5, and the numerous manuscripts of the *Sentences* are examined, loc. cit. and *passim*.

²⁹ Ed. F. S. Schmitt and R. W. Southern, in *Memorials of St. Anselm*, London, 1969, pp. 8 and 13-26.

³⁰ Ibid., pp. 97-102.

³¹ Index, pp. 367-8, for the words *Adulterium, Copulatio, Fornicatio, Sponsus*.

³² p. 103.

³³ 'S. Bernard et la dévotion joyeuse', in *S. Bernard homme d'Église*, Paris, 1953, pp. 237-47.

³⁴ 'A l'école de S. Bernard, De l'humour à l'amour', in *Témoins de la spiritualité occidentale*, Paris, 1965, pp. 264-87.

³⁵ M. Zink, *La prédication en langue romane avant 1300*, Paris, 1976, pp. 182, 374, 386-99.

VI

Champagne as a Garden of Love

In order to make a brief general survey of love literature in twelfth-century France, it would be necessary to make preliminary surveys of restricted areas such as Languedoc and Aquitaine, and literary centres such as Paris, Orléans, Reims, just to mention a few among the many possible ones. In this present chapter I would like merely to open up avenues for further study of a specific region, Champagne. I shall cover a time-span of approximately fifty years, from 1120 to *circa* 1180, during which period this region, with its capital city, Troyes, was a sort of paradise wherein flourished many types of love literature. However, we can truly grasp the spirit of love which thrived in Troyes and its neighbouring parts only if we have in mind the political and social background of the times. A short survey of such a background will, then, be a necessary starting-point.

1. *The castles*

Feudal society in the bailliage of twelfth-century Troyes has been thoroughly studied by Theodore Evergates.[1] The author has not only produced maps showing the growth of economic, political, and religious centres, with particular attention to the riverine regions of the Seine and the Aube, but he also reminds us that St. Bernard had business dealings with the Count of Troyes, Thibaud, and with his family.[2] Several of Bernard's letters still exist as evidence.[3] Evergates lists the religious houses founded during the twelfth century in the bailliage of Troyes.[4]

It is interesting to note that not one of these foundations is a restoration of traditional Benedictine monasticism: six are Cistercian, others are Premonstratensian or canonical. The Paraclete, where Héloïse was a nun, was a complex institutional structure made up of certain elements handed down from the ancient institution of deaconesses—which, let it be said in passing, still exists in the order of the Cesarine nuns, so called because of their connections with St. Cesaire of Arles, and some of whom adopted Carthusian customs—whereas other elements came from Celtic, Benedictine, and Cistercian monasticism.[5] Thus in the region of Troyes there were seven monasteries of what I have already typified in Chapter II as 'traditional' monasticism by the fact that they were recruited mostly among their oblates, and twelve houses of 'new' monasticism, recruited mainly among adults.

The register of the 'fiefs of Champagne' (*feoda Campaniae*) shows that there existed twenty-six castellanies belonging to the Count of Champagne and in them were almost 2,000 knights and lords. A cousin of St. Bernard, Hugh, came from the castellany of Payns. He it was who became the first Master of the Order of Knights Templar and asked his cousin to write the treatise *In Praise of the New Militia*. Within the castellanies it was the duty of each one of the *milites* to fortify the watch-tower and supply military help in the event of an outbreak of hostilities.[6] The members of a dozen or so families were linked together by a network of close and constant relationships by the intermediary of their collateral branches. Among other names one that springs to mind is Jully. St. Bernard drew up the constitutions of a nunnery founded on land belonging to this family.[7] In noble families degrees of rank gradually evolved: the womenfolk shared in the family prestige and were titled Dame—*Domina*—or Damoiselle—*Domicella*.[8]

11. *The synagogue*

Centrally situated in the part of Champagne which interests us, midway between Clairvaux and the Paraclete, was Troyes. It was an important centre of commerce, politics, literature, and religion, endowed with no less than two chapters and three abbeys.[9] A market-town of some importance dealing in wool and textiles, its fairs were renowned throughout Europe and, towards the end of the century, attracted wealthy merchants such as Pietro di Bernadone and his son Francis of Assisi. There were other thriving fairs in the district to which the monks, the majority of whom were probably Cistercians, went to sell their products. It is quite understandable that these fairs held out attractions to certain monks, and more than once general chapters issued edicts on the subject.[10] St. Bernard was fond of using the theme in his everyday sermons: he compared the monk to a merchant who, while going to the fair, encounters the Lord. After much bartering the merchant-monk gives up his wares to his master and is persuaded to return to his monastery. Just as in his sermons the abbot of Clairvaux contrived to sublimate without suppression images of chivalry and love graved in his monk's memories, so did he seek to give new significance to the experiences of trade and fairs. It is in such light that we must interpret the *Parable of a Merchant Monk*, which has come down to us in several redactions and was later to inspire Nicholas of Clairvaux.[11]

Historians have established a connection between Troyes and other centres of commerce, and Jewish communities which, though they were only minor, were thriving, influential, and faithful to their religion. Recent study has revealed the vitality of the synagogues at Reims and Châlons in Champagne.[12] Recent excavation at Rouen has revealed the remains of what appears to have been a Yeshiva or Jewish academy of higher learning dating from the eleventh or twelfth century. There is a certain difference of opinion between scholars as to the exact nature of the building: while some—the majority—maintain that it was in fact an academy, others suggest that it was a synagogue. Whichever it may be, this seems to confirm the existence of Jewish culture in medieval times. It is not impossible that there was also a Yeshiva at Troyes, whose synagogue has been made

famous by Rabbi Shelomo Izhaqui (†1105), also known as Rashi.
He wrote many biblical commentaries which were rapidly cir-
culated. His work was continued by his secretary Shemiah and
a series of rabbis—among whom we may name Joseph Kara,
Rashbam, Rabbenn Tam—who took inspiration from the
method adopted by Rashi and very carefully avoided attacking
Christians.[13] They illustrated the fact that at the beginning of
the twelfth century both Jews and Christians began to have
renewed interest in the Bible. For them 'this spirit of the age
had the result that it stimulated study and scholarship among
the Jews . . . and while Rashi and his disciples were producing
their works, Abelard and St. Bernard were teaching not far from
Troyes, where there was an ecclesiastical school as well, with a
brilliant reputation. At one and the same time that students were
flocking to Rashi, others were coming from all quarters, "leaving
their towns and cities" to sit at the feet of Abelard. Someone like
St. Bernard, with a deeply religious and mystical spirit would
know his Vulgate thoroughly.'[14]

'In Rashi's time too, mystical interpretation of Scripture
began to appear. But although Rashi respected the knowledge of
the Jewish mystics, he did not altogether follow their method. He
was living probably right at the heart of the great devotional
movement that was so evident in St. Bernard.'[15] The works of
this Jewish master have several times been copied, edited, and
translated,[16] especially his commentary on the Song of Songs.[17]
He and others like him, being part of the society in which they
lived, used French as spoken in Champagne dialect, which they
merely transliterated into Hebrew characters.[18] In Rashi's writings we find 'fables'[19] very like those of Peter of Alphonse, a
Spanish Jew who became a Christian in 1106 and borrowed elements from the Muhammadan tradition. In particular Peter
wrote a treatise on the formation of clerics—*Disciplina Clericalis*[20]
—which, very probably, was known to St. Bernard.[21]

Rashi has sometimes been called the 'Sage of Troyes'[22] on
account of his 'sympathetic understanding of human nature',
and it is a tempting thought to consider him as something of a

Jewish St. Bernard: 'his contemporaries seem to have respected him as a man of vast erudition and great vision. Young and old were fascinated not only by his exceptional talent, but the warmth of his personality.'[23] In cases of marital disagreement, particularly, he tended always to indulgence and reconciliation.[24] When he insisted on the literal meaning of the legal prescriptions contained in the Pentateuch, which is both historical and practical in nature, it was his intention, doubtless, to react against the allegorical interpretation given by the Christians.[25] But his commentary on the Song of Songs is very similar to that of most monastic commentators in the twelfth century. The monks interpreted the bride and bridegroom of the Song as the Church and Christ, but for Rashi they represented Israel and God. However, in both instances the symbolism is identical: 'Solomon, under the guidance of the Holy Spirit wrote a book in which he used the literary comparison of a woman doomed to widowhood (with her husband still alive): longing for her husband, leaning upon her lover, remembering her young love for him and confessing her sin. Her lover too, suffers at her suffering, remembering the grace of her youth, her ravishing beauty, and the excellence of her good works. . . . He is her husband still and she, his wife; when the time is ripe he will come back to her.'[26] Many details of the commentary enlarging on this theme are found also in St. Bernard's works.[27] This coincidence is to be explained by the fact that St. Bernard drew inspiration from Origen who had himself consulted the rabbis. A recent and very enlightening translation of the Targum on the Song of Songs[28] shows that commentators had a mine of inspiration from which to draw symbols and reminiscences of the history of the Chosen People. It would seem that this Targum was a common source for the rabbinic schools, Origen, Rashi, and St. Bernard. Anyone who reads this text constantly comes across traditional themes upon which Bernard played his own variations. It has been suggested that the Victorines, Nicholas of Lyre, and other Christian commentators were influenced by Rashi in their exegesis of the Song.[29] Whatever may be the similarities which exist between Rashi and St. Bernard, they are sufficiently explained by the traditional themes found in the Targum and in the works of Origen, who had interpreted the Song as a 'parable' of God's love for his chosen people.[30] Origen appropriated many of the ideas he found in rabbinic literature,[31] and handed them down to Christian authors, St. Bernard and others.[32]

III. *The court*

The preceding few facts about Jewish culture in and around Troyes show that Jews and Christians, noblemen and burghers, townsmen and peasants mingled together and exchanged views. We may ask whether in the district of Troyes there were any Cathars teaching any 'popular heresy'. In the village of Vertus near Châlons[33] there were disciples of a certain Lieutard, many of whom challenged the goodness of marriage and conjugal love.[34] But there does not seem to have been anything similar around Troyes.

The court of Champagne, one of the most prolific literary centres in twelfth-century France, resided in Troyes. Many of its artists are known to us.[35] We have, for example, Nicholas of Clairvaux, a monk of Montiéramey, who was for a short time Bernard's chief secretary.[36] There was also Peter, the abbot of Montier-le-Celle, who dedicated his treatise on *Claustral Discipline* to Count Henry the Liberal,[37] and Philip of Harvengt, a Premonstratensian, who left a commentary on the Song of Songs.[38] In fact there were quite a number of trouvères and poets, the most famous of whom was Chrétien de Troyes.

Among all the splendid works produced at the court of Champagne there is one which deserves our special attention. This is a paraphrase in French verse of Psalm 44, the psalm *Eructavit*, which, like the Song of Songs, is an epithalamium.[39] The author of this long commentary in verse interpreted the psalm as symbolizing the spiritual nuptial union between Christ and his Church. The text, written after St. Bernard's time, leads us to think that the author was dependent on the work of the abbot of Clairvaux.[40] We notice various similarities between the two. For example, Christ's Ascension is likened to a procession during which choirs of angels come to meet their Lord,[41] and the editor of this metrical paraphrase recalls one of St. Bernard's *Parables* in this connection.[42] And this is certainly one of the themes that St. Bernard liked to talk about in his everyday sermons.[43] In other passages, the joy of the Church at Christmas, feast of the Lord's Nativity,[44] and the joy of paradise are described as being the 'joy of the court'[45] of which Chrétien de Troyes speaks at the end of *Erec and Enide*. Military images of chivalry are used—as in the *Parables* and *Sentences* of St. Bernard—with fair abundance, and such imagery is more frequent than that of love. In this poem, written for a certain Countess Marie who lived in those times, the vocabulary of secular love is applied to the mystery of the Incarnation and the response it should call forth from the Church and each individual soul: expressions like *fine amor*, *amors fine*[46] recur frequently and in one manuscript there is the variant *bone amor*.[47] Such disinterested love teaches how to love and rejoice in none but the King:

> File, aime le roi finemant
> Nule rien plus ne te demant.
> Fine amors t'aprandra a feire
> Comant tu li porras miauz plaire;
> Fines amors viennent de lui
> Et fins joie con de celui
> Qui onques d'amer ne se feint
> Ne ne demande fors qu'on l'aint.[48]

At the end of this *Chançon de chambre*[49] the lesson to be retained is set out in one concise sentence:

> Pansez, dame, de bien amer.[50]

IV. *The riddle of Andrew the Chaplain*

May we lawfully bring forward as witness to the love in Champagne the author of a treatise in Latin, *De Amore*, who is referred to in later manuscripts as Andrew, chaplain to the King of France? Such a possibility has been contested.[51] If Andrew was chaplain, why was he at the court of Troyes? When was he writing? And why did he write? These are some of the many questions discussed by the scholars, but what is of interest here is to know what he taught and how much influence he had.

Whatever may have been Andrew's functions, if any, one thing is clear: he had gone through ecclesiastical studies and it is obvious that he intended rewriting for his times and his readers, whoever they may have been, Ovid's *Art of Loving*. This is immediately suggested by the title and the opening lines of his book. Did he intend to write a parody? Or a satire against the clergy? Or, again, a mere amusement for any possible readers? Whatever may be the answers to these questions, the social structures he supposed and described, and which furnish the matter for his teaching, are revealing of the many barriers erected between men and women of those times. From the beginning onwards, everything is based on the difference in social categories: 'Among women, there are the plebs, the noble, others nobler still; and the same applies to men, they are plebeian or noble in varying degrees.'[52] A copyist shows that he had a keen perception of this social segregation and the dawning anti-feminism, when he added this title and gloss: 'Concerning the orders of men and women, and how there is one more order among men than among women'.[53] And in fact, in all that follows, it is never a matter of how man treats woman, but how a man of a given social category treats a woman of a given social category. And we may notice that courtesy (*curialitas*) is identified as the benefit (*bonum*) arising from love.[54] It is usually associated with nobility, without, however, becoming identified with it: courting may go on between people of different orders, but these orders cannot be done away with. Within the order of those who are not nobles, the difference between townsmen and peasants is accentuated: courtesy is 'urbanity', the bland or refined manners considered as being characteristic of town-dwellers as opposed to the 'rusticity' of countrymen.[55] Of course it does happen that a nobleman loves a woman of 'lower order', in which case she hastens to put forward an objection given as being typical of an experience common to all: 'a man of higher rank does not usually love a woman of lower estate; but if he should come to do so he quickly tires of her and despises her on the slightest pretext'. The nobleman has his reply ready: love depends upon each person's liberty and not upon his social status. However, all that follows shows that normally 'equality of order' is a necessary condition, and 'inequality of kind' is an obstacle.[56] Then Andrew, in more than twenty-five pages, gives the highest praise to nobility.[57] Courtesy generally presupposes nobility since it excludes any rusticity.[58]

The order of clerics is also a sort of nobility, coming from God rather than from birth; it is a state of celibacy, but if human weakness should require the choice of a partner in marriage then it is to be determined by social standards, and in particular the safeguard of reputation.[59] 'The peasant order is totally ignorant of courtesy. As for relations with peasant women, desire can be satisfied without any obligations towards them: they may be used even by force of violence, if necessary.'[60] Thus, from the beginning to the end of his treatise, Andrew is a forceful echo of both the barriers separating the orders in society and of the basic difference which makes man superior to woman. This is formulated with cynical energy, towards the end: 'And, even more, whereas in men by reason of the boldness of their sex, excesses in love or lust are to be tolerated, in women, this is to be considered as a crime to be condemned and the ruin of their reputation.'[61] This statement is made after the diversion in which Andrew imagines those astonishing 'courts of love' which are both tribunals and places for discussions in which women appear to have all authority and to decide everything as if they were supreme judges.[62] The irony of such parody bursts out in the last twenty pages of the work, where all the vices are attributed to women.[63] This handbook on love, based from the start on the inequalities which formed an essential part of the society in those days, ends in this way with the most radical and most developed manifesto of anti-feminism written in the twelfth century.

Now, admitting that this text was written in Champagne, did it have any influence at all, particularly in that area? It is preserved in very few manuscripts, and several of them are fourteenth- and fifteenth-century ones. A fragment which could be dated twelfth-century has been found in Italy,[64] where the work was translated in the fourteenth century.[65] Towards the end of the twelfth century the chronicler Lambert of Ardres, writing in Flanders, recounts a weird love story[66] which, the writer says, seems 'like a fable',[67] and which ends with an allusion to a certain 'André of Paris'.[68] Could it be our author who is in question here? There is no evidence to tell us this with any certainty.[69] The first clear references to his treatise appear in the thirteenth century, and in particular in a document dated 1277 in which it is condemned by the bishop of Paris, Etienne Tempier.[70] Fourteen years later a certain Drouart de la Vache criticized it 'disapprovingly', neither he nor two of his friends whom he mentions finding it edifying; far from seeing it as a humorous entertainment, it was for them a source of serious scandal.[71]

At all events, we can no longer simply say that *De Amore* is 'one of the best known works from the second half of the twelfth century, and that it had a rich written tradition':[72] this tradition was poor, and the treatise was better known in the nineteenth and twentieth centuries than in the twelfth. It is indeed, on both these grounds, a mistake to describe the love practised 'in a medieval castle' in the light of this work:[73] firstly, because it presents a picture which was far from being accepted; and again because there is no real reason to think that it enjoyed wide circulation. Whereas St. Bernard's Commentary was what could be called a best-seller, and of which there existed more than a hundred manuscripts dating from his own time, there is not the slightest indication that Andrew the Chaplain was read in Champagne in the twelfth century.

Did Andrew actually know St. Bernard's writings? This is,

a priori, a possibility, since they were numerous. An attempt has been made to prove that he was inspired by the treatise of the abbot of Clairvaux *On the degrees of humility and pride*, but the suggested points of similarity are tenuous and not very convincing.[74] One comparison used by Andrew—that of a fisherman, skilled in drawing and catching fish[75]—does have several parallels in St. Bernard,[76] but it is the sort of commonplace that does not necessarily imply a definite dependence. In short, if we can consider St. Bernard as a product of the garden of love that was twelfth-century Champagne, we can rule out the influence of Andrew the Chaplain.

v. *Héloïse and the Paraclete*

We are confronted by another riddle in the person of Héloïse, a nun of the monastery of the Paraclete. The authenticity of the letters exchanged with Abelard, and in which there is so much mention of love, has been contested and still remains an open question. During a recent discussion on the subject the more experienced of the historians involved hesitated to decide definitely in the affirmative.[77] Yet such would seem a more probable answer to the question in spite of the problems it raises: a decision in the negative would give rise to just as many fresh queries. However, the fact is that the question remains unanswered. Whatever may be, even if letters actually were exchanged between a living Héloïse and Abelard, it might perhaps be more prudent, as we suggested for the works of Andrew the Chaplain, not to take them into consideration since we have no proof of their influence. It is possible that the text of this correspondence had been preserved at the Paraclete, and even copied for daughter houses. But apart from that it does not seem probable that anyone else would have read these letters and taken inspiration from them. One thing is certain, however: the community to which Héloïse belonged adopted the Cistercian liturgy.[78] It is probable too that after Abelard's death St. Bernard was in close touch with the Paraclete and may even have been something of a spiritual director to the nuns.[79] Héloïse and Bernard, each in their own way, were products of the same garden of love.

It would certainly be useful for our purposes to assume that there existed an incomplete text of the correspondence between Abelard and Héloïse, because it contains the elements of every play of love that we find in St. Bernard's *Sermons on the Song*, and in the romance *Erec and Enide* written by Chrétien of Troyes. It would be a satisfying thought to think that these different authors influenced one another. But we must admit that the literary themes we find in their works are archetypes common to all forms of love.

When Abelard acknowledges that his love for Héloïse had caused the dulling of intellectual sharpness, we are reminded of the manner in which Erec came to lose his knightly gallantry. Abelard writes:

It became utterly boring for me to have to go to school, and equally wearisome to remain there and to spend my days on study when my nights were sleepless with love-making. As my interest and concentration flagged, my lectures lacked all inspiration and were merely repetitive; I could do no more than repeat what had been said long ago, and when inspiration did come to me, it was for writing love-songs, not the secrets of philosophy.[80]

And in Chrétien's romance we read:

But Erec loved her [Enide] with such tender love, that he cared no more for arms, nor did he go to tournaments, nor have any desire to joust; but he spent his time cherishing his wife. . . . His friends grieved over this, and often regretted among themselves that he was so deeply in love. Often it was past noon before he left her side.[81]

Then for Erec and Abelard, Enide and Héloïse there came a time of widowhood, as it were, the period when love is purified by becoming separated, disinterested, sublimated love. Needless to say, there are differences in the psychological and spiritual attitudes of these two couples. But throughout their inner and exterior fluctuations there remain, in spite of great dissimilarities, sufferings and joys which are similar because common to every love affair, be it carnal or spiritual. Inevitably our mind comes back to the desolation and consolation expressed by St. Bernard in his *Sermons on the Song*.

VI. *St. Bernard and the Bride of the Song of Songs*

We must now compare the two greatest poets of the garden of love, Champagne. The field of possible research is so wide that we shall have to limit ourselves to one work by each author: for Bernard we shall take his *Sermons on the Song of Songs* and for Chrétien his *Erec and Enide*. These two authors wrote with a common cultural background, influenced by the Bible, and by more or less numerous elements taken from the patristic and liturgical traditions as well as from the classical. It is virtually impossible for Chrétien to have ignored Bernard's *Song of Songs*, which had such immediate and wide circulation. He must have heard about this work, and he may well have read it in Latin, although it could by then have been translated into French. Possibly Chrétien was better versed in classical literature than Bernard yet, on the other hand, Bernard was quite definitely acquainted with the secular love literature of his times.

These facts are sufficient to account for the many and sometimes striking similarities to be found in these two love poets. It would be interesting to illustrate this in the form of a quiz, reading passages first from one then from the other and asking, 'Who wrote that?' It would no doubt come as a surprise to many listeners that the most intimate, intense, and even violent expressions of love experience are to be found, not in the secular poet, writing for a court, but in the monastic poet, writing in Clairvaux. But here the best method will be to go through Bernard's *Song of Songs* and quote some of his hymns to love, and to do the same with Chrétien's *Erec*, calling to mind its main themes, thus enabling us to place this romance in the context of the whole of Chrétien's work, at the same time setting it in the context of the spiritual development common to both human and divine love, in that period and area.

We must take note of the fact that, for poetical and theological writers such as Bernard, William of Saint-Thierry, and
others, love can be experienced both in monastic life and in the
married state: this was never denied by such writers. But
Chrétien's first romance, *Erec*, illustrates, particularly, the
exaltation of conjugal love, and sets the tone for all his subsequent works. It was a common saying among scholars who
studied, in the last decades of the nineteenth century, so-called
courtly love literature, that there was no true love outside
adultery. And of course we have to admit that then, as now, happy
marriages do not make headlines. However, when Chrétien sings
the praise of married love, he mirrors one of the realities of life.

In St. Bernard's *Song of Songs*, the first thing we should note
is that when he wants to speak of God's love for mankind he
chooses to do so by means of the literary theme of a pastoral, in
which a nobleman falls in love with a shepherdess, a girl whose
social standing is beneath his own: 'Behold the bridegroom who
comes leaping upon the mountains. Let us imagine as in a paint-
ing—*pingemus*—a tall man, a man of giant stature, fired with
love for a poor little woman, and imagine that she is absent. He
runs towards her, towards the embrace he desires. He leaps over
the mountains and the hills which rise so far above the earth and
its plains that their peaks sometimes pierce the clouds.'[82]

This text, among many others, explains why Bernard, in the
line of an ancient and uninterrupted spiritual tradition, chose
the Song of Songs from the Bible as the basic text when he wanted
to write about love, a love which, as a phrase taken from secular
love literature says, is an 'amor de longh', love from afar, love
at a distance, separated love: it symbolizes and expresses the
dialectic of presence and absence, a characteristic of Christian
spiritual experience; it speaks of a search, a quest after love, a
'queste d'amour'. And how does Bernard develop this theme?
He makes use of the same devices, images, themes, and sometimes intrigues that we find in secular love literature: jealousy
put to the test, pure love wanting no other reward than itself,
conflict between honour and love.[83] In the first nine sermons,

Bernard gives his commentary on the beginning of the Song of Songs, the first words of the Bride: 'Let him kiss me with the kiss of his mouth.' And in the last text of this series he justifies the appeal that he will make more than once to his imagination in inventing a fictitious dialogue. At first the Bride can only break the silence by short replies; and then she is unable to restrain her expressions of love: 'Let us now, my brethren return to our text and explain the words of the Bride and all that follows. These words, spoken abruptly without the least introduction, hang unsteadily so to speak, and loosely swing in mid-air for want of a beginning or context. It is, therefore, necessary that something be premised to which they may intelligibly cohere. Let us accordingly suppose that those who I have called the friends of the Bridegroom, as yesterday and the day before, so also today have come on a visit to salute the spouse. Finding her discontented and complaining and out of humour, they wonder what the cause can be, and address her in this manner: "What has happened? How is it we see you sadder than usual? Wherefore these unexpected complaints and murmurs? Certainly, after returning at length to your lawful husband, and only when compelled to do so by the ill-treatment of the other lovers after whom you had gone so disloyally and unfaithfully, certainly, you did importune him with prayers and tears to allow you even to kiss his feet. Is it not so?" "Yes," she answers. "What then? Having obtained the request, and the pardon of your infidelities at the same time in the kiss of his foot, did you not again grow discontented? Not satisfied with so much condescension, but desiring greater familiarity, with the same insistence as before you did now implore and obtain the second grace, and with the kiss of his hand were adorned with virtues neither few in number nor little in importance. You admit all this?" "I do," she replies. "Are you not the one who used to protest and promise that, if ever she was admitted to the kiss of his hand, this would be enough for her, and thereafter she would ask for nothing more?" "The same," she confesses. "What then? Perhaps you will complain that some of the graces already bestowed have been taken

back?" "No indeed." "Or, it may be that you are afraid you shall
be called upon to answer for the sins of your past life, which it
was your hope had been forgiven?" "Not even that." "Well
then, tell us what is wrong and how we can help you." "I cannot
rest," she exclaims, "until he kisses me with the kiss of his
mouth. I am thankful for being allowed to kiss his feet. I am
grateful for the privilege of kissing his hand. But if he has any
care for me 'let him kiss me with the kiss of his mouth'. I am not,
I repeat, ungrateful but—I love. What I have already obtained
is, I acknowledge, too much for my desert, yet altogether too
little for my desire. I am governed more by desire than by reason.
Do not, I beg of you, blame my presumption, since affection
urges me on. Modesty remonstrates, but love is supreme. I am
not ignorant that 'the honour of the King loveth judgement'.
But headlong love will not wait for judgement, will not suffer the
restraints of counsel, will not be held in check by modesty, will
not follow the guidance of reason. I beg, I implore, I entreat, 'let
him kiss me with the kiss of his mouth'." [84]

There are so many other passages we could quote, ardently
reflecting on these exclamations of love, with which the Song of
Songs overflows. '"My beloved to me and I to him." There can
be no doubt my brethren, that the mutual love of the Bridegroom
and Bride burns as a fire in this passage. And in that reciprocity
of affection we behold the supreme felicity of the one and the
amazing condescension of the other. For not between equals is
the loving union or embrace here in question. But what is the
gift which the Bride boasts of having, by the privilege of singular
love, received from her Bridegroom and bestowed upon him in
turn? That is a secret which no one can pretend to understand
fully, except those who, by the perfect purity of their souls and
bodies, have deserved to experience something similar in themselves. For it is a mystery of love. Hence it is not by discourse of
reason we are to attain to it, but by conformity of will. [85] "Return,
my beloved," cries the Bride. It is evident that he whom she
thus recalls is not now present, yet has been with her, and that
but a short time ago. For she is calling him back, as it seems,

whilst he is still in the act of retiring. That he is so soon solicited to return is a proof both of the greatness of her love and of the attraction of his lovable person. But who are these fervent votaries of charity? Who are these tireless devotees of love, of whom the one is pursued and the other driven forward by the ungovernable force of affection?[86]

'"In my bed at night I sought him whom my soul loves." The Bridegroom evidently has not returned at the desire and solicitation of her who recalled him. Wherefore? In order that her desire may increase, that she may give proof of her love, that she may be the longer occupied in the exercise of charity. The delay consequently is no evidence of anger on the part of the Beloved, it is in fact nothing more than pious dissimulation. It only remains, therefore, to seek him, if perchance he may be found when sought, who when called has deferred to come.'[87]

Further on, Bernard explains these words of the Bride to the watchmen: '"Have you seen him who my soul loves?" O love, so precipitate, so violent, so ardent, so impetuous, suffering the mind to entertain no thought but of yourself, spurning everything, despising everything which is not yourself, content with yourself alone. You disturb all order, disregard all usage, ignore all measure. You triumph over, in yourself, and reduce to captivity whatever appears to belong to fittingness, to reason, to decorum, to prudence, or to counsel. Thus every thought which this bride thinks and every word which she utters savours of you and sounds of you and of nothing but you, so completely have you monopolized both her heart and her tongue. She says to the watchmen, "Have you seen him whom my soul loves?" As if she expected them to know what she is thinking of. Do you inquire concerning him whom your soul loves? And has he no other name except this? But who are you yourself and who is he? Such questions, my brethren, I should be inclined to ask on account of the strangeness of the language and the remarkable disregard for the proprieties of speech which appear to distinguish this part of Holy Scripture from every other. Therefore it seems to me that in examining this nuptial song we ought to attend more to the affection than to the verbal expression. And the reason is because holy love, which is manifestly the sole, exclusive theme of the entire composition, can be measured "not in word or in tongue, but in deed and in truth". It is love that is speaking everywhere. And should any of you desire to attain to an understanding of the things which he reads, let him love. For it is useless for him who loves not to attempt to read or to listen to this Canticle of love, because the "ignited word" can obtain no lodging in a heart that is cold and frozen. Just as he who knows not Greek cannot understand one who is speaking Greek, just as one who knows not Latin cannot understand one speaking Latin, and so on with all other tongues: in the same way to him who knows not love, the language of love is barbarous and becomes as "sounding brass or a tinkling cymbal". But these, I mean the watchmen who keep the city, having themselves also received from the Spirit the gift of love, are able to comprehend what the same Spirit speaks; and as the language of holy love is perfectly familiar to them, they can answer immediately in the same tongue, that is, by loving affections and offices of piety.'[88]

The last sermons rise to a crescendo, when it is a question of extolling conformity of will, which makes lovers not only equal—following the definition of Cicero[89]—but united and even 'one' as St. Paul teaches. This lengthy exposition warrants the long extracts given here: poetry and ardour go side by side with a theology which is at the same time exact and profound:

'It is by this conformity of charity, my brethren, that the soul is wedded to the Word, when, namely, loving even as she is loved, she exhibits herself in her will conformed to him to whom she is already conformed in her nature. Therefore, if she loves him perfectly she has become his bride. What can be more sweet than such a conformity? What can be more desirable than this charity by which, happy soul, not content any longer with human teachers, you are enabled of yourself to draw nigh with confidence to the Word, to cleave to him steadfastly, to interrogate him familiarly and to consult him in all your doubts, as audacious in your desires as you are capacious in your understanding? This is in truth the alliance of a holy and spiritual marriage. But it is saying too little to call it an alliance: it is rather an embrace. Surely we have then a spiritual embrace when the same likes and dislikes make one spirit out of two? Nor is there any occasion to fear lest the inequality of the persons should cause some defect in the harmony of wills, since love knows nothing of reverence. Love means an exercise of affection, not an exhibition of honour. Honour is given by him who is awe-stricken, who is astounded, who is terrified, who is filled with admiration. But none of these emotions has any place in the lover. Love is all-sufficient for itself. Whithersoever love comes, it subjugates and renders captive to itself all the other affections. Consequently the soul that loves, simply loves and knows nothing else except love. The Word is indeed one who deserves to be honoured, who deserves to be admired and wondered at; yet he is better pleased to be loved. For he is the bridegroom and the soul is his bride, and between a bridegroom and his bride what other relation or connection would you look for except the bond of mutual love? Such is the strength of this bond that it overcomes even the most intimate union which nature forms, I mean the union between parent and child. So much is evident from the words of the Saviour, "For this cause shall a man leave father and mother and shall cleave to his wife." You perceive, my brethren, how love, as it is found between a bridegroom and bride, is not only more powerful than the other human affections but it is even more powerful than itself.

'It must also be remembered that this bridegroom is not only loving but is love itself. May it be likewise said of him that he is honour? You are at liberty to think so, if you choose, but there is no authority for this to be found in Holy Scripture. I have read therein that "God is love", but never that he is honour or dignity. Not that God does not demand honour, for he has said, "If I be a father, where is my honour?" But it is as Father that he speaks thus. Were he to speak in his character as a bridegroom, I believe he would use different language and would say, "If I be a bride-groom, where is my love?" For he has asked the same question concerning the reverence due to him in his capacity as Lord, "If I be a master, where is my fear?" God therefore requires to be honoured as a Father, to be feared as a Lord, but to be loved as a bridegroom. Now in these various affections what is that which appears to excel and to hold the pre-eminent position? Doubtless it is love. For without love "fear has pain" and honour finds no favour. Fear is slavish until it has been emancipated by love. And the honour which proceeds not from love better deserves to be called flattery than honour. To God alone are due honour and glory; but God will refuse to accept both the one and the other unless they are sweetened with the honey of love. Love is sufficient of itself, it pleases of itself and for its own sake. It counts as merit to itself and is its own reward. Besides itself love requires no motive and seeks no fruit. Its fruit is its enjoyment of itself. I love because I love and I love for the sake of loving. A great thing, my brethren, is love, if yet it returns to its principle, if it is restored to its origin, if it finds its way back again to its fountain-head, so that it may be thus enabled to continue to flow with an unfailing current. Amongst all the emotions, sentiments, and feelings of the soul, love stands distinguished in this respect, that in the case of it alone has the creature the power to correspond and to make a return to the Creator in kind, though not in equality. For instance, if God is true, "the honour of the king loves judgement", as the psalmist says; but the love of the bridegroom who is love requires of his bride nothing more than a return of love and loyalty. Let her then who is so beloved by him be careful to reciprocate his love. How indeed, can she help loving since she is a bride, and the bride of Love? Or how is it possible that Love should not be loved?

'Rightly therefore does the bride, renouncing all other feelings, abandon herself entirely to love alone, since in the interchange of love she has to correspond to a bridegroom who is Love itself. This, however, is quite certain: he loved her long before she began to love him, and he loves her far more than she loves him. Happy the bride who has deserved to be prevented with the blessing of such exceeding sweetness.'[90]

Eventually, in the final passages, comes the confirmation that disinterested love ranks higher even than fruitfulness itself: 'Not in the same manner is the spiritual mother affected when she is occupied in bringing forth the fruit of souls to the Word, as when she is thus enjoying his caresses. It is purely out of solicitude for her neighbour and his necessities that she devotes herself to the former employment; to the latter she is invited by the sweetness of the Word. As a mother she rejoices in her offspring; but greater are the delights she experiences as a bride in the arms of her bridegroom. Dear to her heart are her children, the precious pledges of conjugal love; but she finds more pleasure in the embraces of her husband. It is good for her to be helping many to salvation; but it is something far sweeter to be transported out of herself and united to the Word. But when does this happen? And how long does it last? It is an intercourse of love most delightful to experience, but it is as rare as it is delightful, and as short-lived as rare.'[91]

Can we wonder that language at once so realistic and so sublime immediately brought forth a resounding echo? For the period of less than a century after it was written there were extant, despite many possibilities of destruction and disappearance, 111 manuscripts, scattered from north to south, from east to west in medieval Europe.[92] While Bernard was alive, his masterpiece influenced a whole literature; and, a little after his death, it was translated, and continued to exercise an influence on the liturgy, on art and iconography, even on the wording of charters and official documents.[93] Bernard was recognized and proclaimed as the greatest poet and minstrel of love Champagne had ever produced.

VII. *Erec and Enide*

Let us now turn to Chrétien's romance on conjugal love, bearing in mind that *Erec and Enide* is the beginning of all his works: faithfulness in conjugal love is a recurrent theme in all his subsequent romances, and this fidelity reaches its climax in his

Yvain. In all Chrétien's writings we find the theme of love allied
with that of the self-denial which is necessary if there is to be any
fidelity between married lovers.

The chronology of Chrétien's life and works has been the
object of constant research. In a very erudite study, which came
out in 1973, Karl Bertau placed the varying stages of the redactions of *Erec* as appearing in the period between 1164 and 1170.[94]
In a later work Claude Luttrell suggested that Chrétien's literary
beginnings should be dated some years later.[95] Be that as it may,
it seems accepted that *Erec* was written for a special occasion, the
investiture of Geoffrey, son of Henry II, as duke of Bretagne. But
Chrétien evidently has not been constrained in his treatment of
it by external pressures. Geoffrey was engaged to Constance,
daughter of Cono of Brittany, and the two were still children
at this time. Chrétien took a simple adventure story and reshaped
it with the help of his studies, chiefly Virgil, Lucan, and Ovid.
The marriage of Erec and Enide is tested through the vicissitudes
they undergo, when their excessive love-making arouses
criticism. A crisis arises when Enide expresses her sorrow at the
change which has come over her husband and caused his different
attitude to be talked of in public. In the composition of the
romance this is a significant part of the poet's creation. It would
be possible to point out in *Erec* many sources which might well
come from Ovid and other classical poets, as well as from the
Bible and Christian literary tradition.[96] But this *Quellenforschung*
could mislead us, because Chrétien knew less about these possible sources than present-day scholars tend to say. *Erec* has been
submitted to sophisticated structural analysis and this has been
very enlightening. But we should probably be more akin to
Chrétien's frame of mind, and that of his public, were we to read
him more naïvely.

Even though some precise texts of Augustine and others on the
process of conversion and inner renewal may have been present
to Chrétien's mind, it is evident that these two themes belong to
the biblical tradition of both the Old and New Testaments, and
they form the basic structure of the whole story. Even if Chrétien

was not a Jew, as some historians have thought, the presence of this biblical background is quite understandable. In fact, the life of adventure upon which Erec sets out is a long testing time. These adventures also involve his wife, and it is only after these are over that Chrétien claims to have shown the reasons for his conduct and the interpretation of it. They emerge triumphant so that their relationship is rebuilt on sound principles and their love is subordinated to the demands of the community in which they are placed. Before the Epilogue a digression takes place; an episode called the 'joie de la cort' is inserted, and it depicts a knight enthralled by a beautiful girl and subservient to her wishes. The immoral aspect of this liaison is intended to highlight the change which has come over the love relationship of hero and heroine. Erec's victory over the obsessed knight confirms his victory over self in the course of the romance.

We could now go through *Erec* as we did Bernard's *Song of Songs*, but let it suffice to notice that from *Eric* to *Yvain*, wherever the hero passes through a series of adventures which lead to the reconciliation of husband and wife, and where Yvain regains sovereignty as the husband, and in the unfinished *Conte du Graal* we see the reconciliation of love for woman with love for the Deity. Here we have a complete religion of love: the worship of an adored lady finds its roots in the Bible and in spiritual writers. The poet was constantly attempting to illustrate the effect that love could have on human behaviour, whether this love be divine or human.

We notice, then, that between Chrétien and Bernard and their sources there exists something more than certain literary parallels and possible interdependence. There seems to be much of Bernard in Chrétien and vice versa. Perhaps it would be true to say that there is much which is common to both as well as to many other writers, with or without direct mutual influence. This is surely due to the fact of universal human experience, the presence of archetypes embedded in the personal and collective memory of all human beings, a common inspirational source of the love symbols in literature the world over—in all civilizations, including that of the Bible. Over and beyond any learning that Bernard and Chrétien may have possessed—not to mention their historians—over and above the immediate knowledge they may have had of literary sources, there exist two fundamental ones: the human psyche and God present within it, at work within and speaking from without through the medium of Holy Writ. In fact, Bernard and Chrétien knew of only one literary tradition, that stemming from the Bible, liturgy, patristic writings, and the Latin classical authors. Bernard depends more on the Bible and Cicero, Chrétien more on Virgil, Lucan, and Ovid.

But both a monk like Bernard and a professional poet such as Chrétien were trying to get over the same truth: there is but one love. There may be a variety of experiences of this love, with God and the human community, or with God, a wife, and the human community. Some of their readers had experienced this variety, others knew only its unity. But these monastic poets and these poetic monks, so to speak, appear to agree on the oneness of love, over and beyond its varieties.

[1] T. Evergates, *Feudal Society in the Bailliage of Troyes under the Counts of Champagne 1152-1284*, The Johns Hopkins University Press, Baltimore-London, 1975.

[2] Ibid., p. 5.

[3] References in the collective work, *Bernard de Clairvaux*, Paris, 1953, p. 653.

[4] Evergates, p. 8.

[5] '"Ad ipsam sophiam Christum." Le témoignage monastique d'Abélard', *Revue d'ascétique et de mystique*, 46 (1970), pp. 161-82.

[6] List of *milites*, in Evergates, p. 61; geographical map of castellanies, p. 62; table of watch-towers, p. 64. We could apply to the castles of Champagne much of what has been written about those of Germany in *Die Burgen im deutschen Sprachraum. Ihre Rechts- und Verfassungsgeschichtliche Bedeutung*, Sigmaringen, 1976.

[7] Jully is quoted in Evergates, p. 103. The 'Statutes of Jully' are edited in *Études sur S. Bernard*, pp. 192-4.

[8] List of 'Fief Holders' with titles of each of them, Evergates, p. 92. See Ch. V, 'The Aristocracy. Counts, Lords and Knights', pp. 96 ff.; list of the 'twelve families', p. 109; on the prestige of women, pp. 130-1.

[9] Geographical map of religious houses, Evergates, p. 9.

[10] References in J. M. Canivez, *Statuta Capitulorum Generalium Ordinis Cisterciensis*, vol. VIII, *Indices*, Louvain, 1941, p. 364, at the word *Nundinae*. On Clairvaux and the fairs of Champagne, *Bernard de Clairvaux*, pp. 112-13.

[11] A text of the parable is edited in *S. Bernardi opera*, VI. 2, pp. 295-303; on the different redactions, cf. *Études sur S. Bernard*, pp. 144-7, and H. Rochais, 'Complément aux paraboles de S. Bernard', *Cîteaux*, 13 (1962), pp. 277-80. The theme was also developed by Nicholas of Clairvaux, *P.L.* 144. 830-9, and by Galland of Régny, in a

work dedicated to St. Bernard, ed. J. Châtillon, 'Gallandi Regniacensis Libellus Proverbiorum. Le recueil de proverbes glosés du cistercien Galland de Regny', *Revue du moyen âge latin*, 9 (1953), pp. 64-5, no. 70.

¹² On the Jewish communities of medieval Champagne: *Rashi*, collected works, with introduction by M. Sperber, Paris, 1974, pp. 33-78; A. Grabois, 'The "Hebraica veritas" and Jewish-Christian Intellectual Relations in the Twelfth Century', *Speculum*, 50 (1975), pp. 613-34; H. Hailperin, *Rashi and the Christian Scholars*, University of Pittsburgh Press, pp. 17-19, 268-9; on Troyes in particular, pp. 74-8; *Rashi. His Teachings and Personality*, *Essays on Occasion of the 850th Anniversary of his Death*, ed. S. Federbusch, New York, 1958, pp. 74-8; R. Chazon, *Medieval Jewry in Northern France. A Political and Social History*, The Johns Hopkins University Press, Baltimore-London, 1973, p. 10, with bibliography, and *passim*: the key communities of French Jewry were Troyes, then Reims; in the Index, p. 238, Troyes is the most frequently cited town. The author also points out, following other writers, the bonds which existed between the Jews of Troyes and its neighbourhood on the one hand, and, on the other, the feudal barony of the region, pp. 29, 62, and *passim*. On the Jewish community in Reims: M. Bur, 'La Champagne féodale', in *Histoire de la Champagne*, published under the direction of M. Crubelier, Toulouse, 1975, p. 151. See also Eugene J. Weintraub, *Chrétien's Jewish Grail: A New Investigation of the Imagery and Significance of the Grail Episode Based upon Medieval Hebraic Sources* (North Carolina Studies in the Romance Languages and Literatures, Essays, No. 2, Chapel Hill, 1976).

¹³ Hailperin, pp. 27-8, 113, 164.

¹⁴ Ibid., p. 24.

¹⁵ Ibid., p. 32.

¹⁶ B. Blumenkranz, G. Dahan, and S. Kerner, *Auteurs juifs en France médiévale. Leur œuvre imprimée*, Toulouse, 1975.

¹⁷ Ibid., p. 110.

¹⁸ *Rashi*, ed. M. Sperber, pp. 123-38; other examples in H. J. Mathews, 'Anonymous Commentary on the Song of Songs. Edited from a unique manuscript in the Bodleian Library', in *Festschrift . . . zum 80ᵉⁿ Geburtstag Moritz Steinschneider*, 1896, p. 239.

¹⁹ *Rashi*, ed. Federbusch, pp. 87-8.

²⁰ Cf. *The 'Disciplina Clericalis' of Petrus Alphonsi*, translated and edited by E. Hermes. Translated into English by P. R. Quarrie, London-Henley, 1977.

²¹ In an *Introduction to the Sentences and to the Parables*, forthcoming in the Latin and Italian editions of the works of St. Bernard, I have indicated the possible connections between Peter of Alphonse and St. Bernard.

²² *Rashi*, ed. Federbusch, pp. 87-8.

²³ Ibid., p. 87.

²⁴ Ibid., pp. 88-9.

²⁵ Hailperin, p. 33.

²⁶ Ibid., p. 241.

²⁷ Cf., for example, ibid., pp. 24, 365, and *passim*.

²⁸ U. Neri, *Il Cantico dei cantici. Antica interpretazione ebraica*, Rome, 1976.

²⁹ *Rashi*, ed. M. Sperber, *passim*; Hailperin, *passim*, and especially B. Smalley, *The Study of the Bible in the Middle Ages*, Oxford, 1952, pp. 149-72.

³⁰ N. de Lange, *Origen and the Jews. Studies in Jewish-Christian relations in Third Century Palestine*, Cambridge, 1976, p. 112.

³¹ Examples in connection with the Song are given in ibid., pp. 60, 67, 81, 115-16, 182, 224.

³² On the presence of Origen in the library of Clairvaux, and on Bernard's dependence on Origen, especially in connection with the Song, see references given above, Ch. IV, n. 26.

[33] *Historiarum lib. II*, XI. 22, ed. M. Prou, *Raoul Glaber. Les cinq livres de ses histoires* (*900-1044*), Paris, 1886, p. 49; it is there reported that Lieutard 'sent away his wife, divorcing as by virtue of some evangelical precept', but no doctrine on marriage is attributed to him.

[34] R. I. Moore, *The Birth of Popular Heresy*, London, 1975, p. 2 and *passim*, and Index, p. 162: 'Abstinence from sexual relations'; p. 163: 'Church: The marriage'.

[35] J. F. Benton, 'The Court of Champagne as a Literary Center', *Speculum*, 36 (1961), pp. 551–91.

[36] Ibid., pp. 555–7; *Recueil d'études*, I, pp. 47–82.

[37] *La spiritualité de Pierre de Celle (1115-1183)*, Paris, 1946; Benton, pp. 557–8; critical edition of *De disciplina* by G. de Martel, Paris, 1977.

[38] Benton, pp. 575–6.

[39] Ibid., pp. 566–7.

[40] Ed. T. Atkinson Jenkins, '*Eructavit*', *an Old French Metrical Paraphrase of Psalm XLIV . . . attributed to Adam de Perseigne*, Dresden, 1909. The attribution of this text to the Cistercian Adam de Perseigne has been accepted by J. Bouvel, 'Biographie d'Adam de Perseigne', in *Collectanea Ord. Cist. Ref.*, 20 (1958), pp. 8–19.

[41] ll. 471–2, p. 21.

[42] p. xxiii.

[43] *Études sur S. Bernard*, pp. 68–9.

[44] l. 34, p. 2.

[45] l. 66, p. 4.

[46] ll. 1439, 1441, p. 63; 1469, p. 64.

[47] p. 63, in the apparatus at ll. 1439 and 1443.

[48] ll. 1443–50, p. 63.

[49] l. 2075, p. 91.

[50] l. 2081, p. 91.

[51] Benton, pp. 578–82; 'The Evidence for Andreas Capellanus Re-examined Again', *Studies in Philology*, 59 (1962), pp. 471–8.

[52] *Andreae Capellani regii Francorum De amore libri tres*, ed. E. Trojel, Copenhagen, 1892, p. 18.

[53] Ibid., in the apparatus.

[54] p. 34.

[55] The words and concepts of urbanity, curiality, and rusticity recur frequently, pp. 106, 127, 155, 159, 205, 207, 241, etc.

[56] p. 114.

[57] pp. 124–50.

[58] pp. 159–60.

[59] pp. 219–24, 248.

[60] p. 235.

[61] p. 324.

[62] pp. 295–312.

[63] pp. 338–58.

[64] The manuscript has been identified by E. Franceschini, *Aevum*, 26 (1952), pp. 81–2.

[65] On the manuscript tradition and translations see, in addition to the Introduction of Trojel's edition: N. de Paepe, in *Levense Bijdragen*, 53 (1964), pp. 120–47; 'M. H. L.' in *Revue d'histoire ecclésiastique*, 43 (1948), p. 765; in *Mélanges offerts à René Crozet*, Poitiers, 1966, II, pp. 921–7; R. Bossuat, art. 'André le Chapelain', in *Dictionnaire des lettres françaises*, published under the direction of G. Grente, *Le moyen âge*, Paris, 1966, p. 55.

[66] *Chronicles of the Counts of Guines*, in *MGH, SS* 24, p. 568. 4–16.

[67] Ibid., in note.

[68] 'Alterum Andream exhibens Parisiensem.'

[69] That is the conjecture of the editor of Lambert of Ardres, loc. cit. The problem has been touched on by Trojel, 'André de Paris et André le Chapelain', *Romania*, 18 (1889), pp. 473-7.

[70] H. S. Denifle and A. Châtelain, *Chartularium Universitatis Parisiensis*, I, Paris, 1889, p. 543. On the circumstances in which Andrew the Chaplain was condemned by Etienne Tempier, on 7 March 1277, at the same time as the philosopher Siger of Brabant and other authors considered as against faith and morals: F. van Steenberghen, *Maître Siger de Brabant*, Louvain-Paris, 1977, pp. 149-51.

[71] B. N. Sargent, 'A Medieval Commentary on Andreas Capellanus', *Romania*, 94 (1973), pp. 528-41. Cf. also D. R. Bustruff, 'The Comedy of Coquetry in Andreas' "De amore"', *Classical Folia*, 28 (1974), pp. 181-90.

[72] Franceschini, loc. cit.

[73] J. F. Gies, *Life in a Medieval Castle*, New York, 1974, pp. 87-90.

[74] R. J. Schoeck, 'Andreas Capellanus and St. Bernard of Clairvaux; The Twelve Rules of Love and the Twelve Steps of Humility', *Modern Language Notes*, 66 (1951), pp. 295-300.

[75] Cited ibid., p. 297.

[76] A. Dimier, *S. Bernard, pêcheur de Dieu*, Paris, 1953.

[77] J. Monfrin, according to S. V. Rovighi, 'Un dibattito sull'autenticità dell epistolario di Abelardo ed Eloisa', *Aevum*, 50 (1976), pp. 357-9. The type of problems raised, and possible solutions, have been dealt with by J. F. Benton, 'The Style of the "Historia calamitatum": A Preliminary Test of the Authenticity of the Correspondence Attributed to Abelard and Heloise', *Viator*, 6 (1975), pp. 59-86, by P. Dronke, *Abelard and Heloise in Medieval Testimonies*, University of Glasgow Press, 1976, and by P. Zerbi, 'Un recente dibattito sull'autenticità della "Historia Calamitatum" e della corrispondenza fra Abelardo ed Eloisa', in *Studi di letteratura e di studi in memoria di Antonio di Pietro*, Milan, 1977, pp. 3-43.

[78] C. Waddell is preparing a study which will show this; I am grateful to him for having communicated the essence of his results. He had already broached the subject under the title 'Peter Abelard's "Letter 10" and Cistercian Liturgical Reform', in *Studies in Medieval Cistercian History*, II, Kalamazoo, 1976, pp. 75-86.

[79] This is J. F. Benton's opinion. I thank him for having spoken to me of it.

[80] *Historia Calamitatum*, trans. B. Radice, *The Letters of Abelard and Heloise*, Penguin Classics, 1974, p. 68.

[81] Trans. W. W. Comfort, *Chrétien de Troyes, Arthurian Romances*, London, 1968, p. 32.

[82] *S. Bernardi opera*, II, p. 97.

[83] It is particularly to be noticed with what frequency Bernard contrasts honour and love: the problem of their difficult reconciliation was one of the basic themes of Chrétien de Troyes and his followers, as has been shown by J. M. Ferrante, *The Conflict of Love and Honor: The Medieval Tristan Legend in France, Germany and Italy*, Paris-The Hague, 1973. Fairly close parallels between the language of love in St. Bernard and in the troubadours have been suggested by J. Deroy, 'Thèmes et termes de la fin'amor dans les Sermones super cantica canticorum de Saint Bernard de Clairvaux', in *Actes du XIIIᵉ Congrès international de Linguistique et Philologie romanes*, Université de Laval, Quebec, 1971, Canada, 1976, pp. 853-67.

[84] Sermon 9. 1-2; the translations given hereafter reproduce with occasional modifications that by A. Luddy, *St. Bernard's Sermons on the Canticle of Canticles, Translated from the Original Latin by a Priest of Mount Mellary*, 2 vols., Dublin, 1920, I, pp. 68-9.

[85] Sermon 67. 8, Luddy, II, p. 288.

[86] Sermon 74. 7, Luddy, II, p. 373.

[87] Sermon 75. 1, Luddy, II, p. 387.

[88] Sermon 79. 1, Luddy, II, pp. 435–6.

[89] See above, p.

[90] Sermon 83. 3–6, Luddy, II, pp. 487–91.

[91] Sermon 85. 13, Luddy, II, p. 520.

[92] *S. Bernardi opera*, I, Introduction, p.. xxiii–xxxi.

[93] *Recueil d'études*, I, pp. 175–92.

[94] K. Bertau, *Deutsche Literatur im europäischen Mittelalter*, Munich, 1973, pp. 1323–7.

[95] C. Luttrell, *The Creation of the First Arthurian Legend. A Quest*, London, 1974, pp. 251–63.

[96] H. Laurie, *Two Studies on Chrétien de Troyes*, Geneva, 1972; R. J. Cormier, *One Heart and One Mind: the Rebirth of Virgil's Hero in Medieval French Romance*, University of Mississippi, 1972. I thank these two authors for having shared with me, both in conversation and by letter, their knowledge of Chrétien.

VII

Epilogue. Bernard and Dante: The Bride and Beatrice

IN Dante's work, as is well known, the doctrine and the person of St. Bernard are both present in various ways. The great Italian poet uses the great French abbot's widely different teaching on politics and Mariology, just to mention two of the many other topics found in Bernard's writings. More important, however, is Bernard's presence in the last and most sublime Canto of the *Divine Comedy*. The influence he had on Dante is witnessed to in the many instances where his texts were very obviously Dante's source of inspiration for ideas and images. It has, for example, been proved that he had read and used at least one of Bernard's *Sermons on the Song of Songs*.[1] There existed between these two authors a certain kinship of poetic thought and experience which they most beautifully express when they write of womankind in love.

In these last few pages I would like to sketch very briefly the basic structural similarity between Bernard and Dante and then go on to illustrate some of the ways they had in common of writing about love and the feminine on the grounds of literary and psychological conceptual categories.

1. *Love and women*

The key word to Dante's entire work is *love*. The last stanza of the *Divine Comedy*[2] speaks of love, and it is this which confers on the whole work a oneness, continuity, and consistency concerning the single major issue: the importance of love. However,

long before this apotheosis, even in the *Inferno*, Beatrice's first
word was for love: 'Love moved me and makes me speak.'³ And
she it is who leads Dante on to love of God,⁴ love consummated
in ecstatic contemplation.⁵ The model and master—literally the
Dottore—of such sublime love is our Bernard. Sitting at the feet
of such a master, Dante learned and proclaimed that this experience is inexpressible. But love will out, and under its pressure, unable to contain himself, he bursts out in prayer addressed
to the greatest of all womankind. His prayer to Mary is a hymn
of love and a hymn to love.⁶ We assist, in the *Comedy*, at a progression from love for Beatrice to love for God; from Beatrice's
expression of love for God to Bernard's. Both authors symbolize
this lofty love: their common symbol is the Bride of the Song of
Songs. The two see the perfect image of this love in the Church:
'The fair bride that was won with the lance and the nails.'⁷ Before
writing his great *Comedy*, Dante composed many love poems: in
the *Rime* and the *New Life*, in all his works there are more than
twenty allusions to Solomon considered either as a king or a
lover. It is significant, too, that the women of whom Dante speaks
are often symbols of the love of God, as is the Bride in the Song.

The Bride is used then, by both Bernard and Dante, as a
symbol of a more than human love. Furthermore, woman is a
model of the Church, the perfect Bride of Christ. At the end of
Bernard's last completed Sermon on the Song of Songs we find
the same theme of ecstatic, inexpressible love as in the final
stages of the *Paradiso*: where words fail, experience alone can
relate what it is to be one spirit with God in perfect union. Dante
writes: 'O how scant is speech and how feeble to my conception
. . . had not my mind been smitten by a flash wherein came its
wish.'⁸ And Bernard: 'What takes place between God and me I
can feel but not express.'

11. *Two similar processes: personification and sublimation*

Let us now go more into detail about this similarity of experience
and expression as seen in Bernard and Dante. To this end it will

be interesting and rewarding to examine two processes they had in common and which they both used at two different levels: the surface level of literary expression; the deeper level of psychic experience and spiritual interpretation. These two levels, of course, cannot be dissociated, but for the sake of argument it is necessary to make distinctions. The processes may aptly be called personification of love and transfiguration of woman.

Though personification is a constant feature of love literatures, its meaning and function vary from one author to another. When a poet, Bernard and Dante among others, speaks to love personified of the love burning within himself, the personification is in fact this love externalized. The poet thereby distances himself with regard to his own emotion and the object of his affection in order to contemplate it and enter into sweet commerce with it. The resulting effect is to transform the loved love and intensify the poet's awareness of it. To converse sweetly with Love personified is not only to be in love with Love, but also to know it and become increasingly aware of it. Love is thus expressed and accepted, understood and assumed by the poet, who mounts gradually in this way to fuller, more personal, lucid, and courageous identification with his own inner *affectus*. Such a process is necessary in order that love be transformed from an enslaving passion, passively suffered, to a liberating and liberated virtue, a dynamic force compelling to rational and conscious activity: man enslaved to love vegetates; man liberated by love acts.

This happy state implies that a man's rational self has submitted his emotions to the keenest of his volitional and intellectual powers. In this way, for example, striving for justice, a rational reality, implies a motivation grounded in the emotional experience of the evils of injustice. In the personification of love, the process allows a man to distance himself from the purely emotional passion and personalize it on the higher rational level. It is precisely this that we find in Bernard and in Dante. Both are Christian mystics, to a lesser or greater extent, and as such have experienced a self-subsistent, quite other reality: God, the absolute of love, absolute Love: 'The love that moves the sun and the other stars.'[9] This is the expression of sublimated love.

It is frequent for the love relationship to be expressed in terms of relationship with woman. Thus, in the process of sublimating love, it is woman who is gradually transformed too. Before going further, let us clarify the meaning given to 'sublimation'. In the present context we take it to signify purification, the passage from a lower to a high plane of reality. This is the traditional, pre-Freudian sense of the terms. Likewise, the use of the word 'idealization' does not imply something fictitious, beyond the realm of reality. Human feelings, passions, emotions, especially those of love, are very real and should not be suppressed. They must, quite to the contrary, be pressed into service. To be of lasting value, the affections of love must be transformed. We may therefore, quite reasonably, speak of a process of transformation, transfiguration, transposition, all so many words evoking—by reason of the prefix—a 'beyond'. Love and lovers constantly seek a comprehension—an intellectual grasping—of both self and the other. In Bernard and Dante it is woman who is presented as having best seized love: 'women who have the understanding of love'.[10]

This feminine ability to comprehend love is diversely represented. Frequently, the poet Dante speaks of love to a woman; more frequently in Bernard's works, it is a woman in love who speaks in the name of men in love. Both approaches are revealing of man and his emotions, for they give us a glimpse of male reactions to love and to the feminine, womankind taken as the object or the symbol of love. Women in such contexts are merely means to an end: they are the channel by which flow the poet's own sentiments about love. Therefore it matters but little from a historical point of view who such women really were, or whether they actually did exist. Dante's commentators vary in opinion: the women who figure in his works—perhaps even Beatrice herself—were either historical figures or purely symbolic; Dante moved in the realm of either *eros* or *agape*. Who can say? Yet is it impossible that these women were both historical and symbolic? Is it not the special gift of poets and mystics to transform everything and everyone they touch, enhancing their beauty in a re-creation? Surely woman is no exception? Such artistic transformation transfigures woman in the poetic, mystic vision and gives her a higher and more noble form, something beyond the ken of us poor mortals.

> Thou, Violetta, in more than mortal form.[11]
> I beheld flying in haste a sweet angel of love.[12]
> Coming from heaven and returning to heaven
> I was of heaven and thither shall return.[13]
> Love who dost launch thy power from the heavens.[14]

III. *Two similar results: renunciation and integration*

The return to heaven symbolizes death. Through death, over and beyond death, separated lovers are reunited, and their reunion is always more sublime than their union here on earth. There come to mind the words uttered by one of Gabriel Marcel's heroes: 'It is as if you had been given back to me again after you had died.'[15] In love literature, that of the courts, the mystics, and also in Dante's, sublimation is a new form of fidelity: separation and death are the cause and the condition of desire which is a higher form of possession. Love literature in all its forms, and each in its own way, expresses the same tension, straining forward to the loved one, with its concomitant inability to achieve, here below, full and definitive satisfaction in love.

There is no sublimation without foregoing humiliation, no transfiguration without preceding disfiguration, no transformation without deformation, no new life—*vita nuova*—without death. Therefore the way to being and to joy on a higher plane, to true resurrection, passes through the valley of renunciation, serenely accepted suffering. Renunciation of immediate satisfaction in love is a sacrifice leading to fuller satisfaction of desire in the end. Such self-renunciation is not easy: it does not go without temptation to grasp satisfaction at a baser price. However, when, and if, emotional resistance is overcome by the acceptance of rational norms, values, modes of experience and existence, the process leads to a rewarding and peaceful integration of the emotional and the rational, of real human love and real divine love. The result is a synthesis of the symbol and the reality of love, a synthesis which occurs when human desires and emotional longings support the rational need for God, thus introducing consistency between the carnal and the rational self.

This integration is achieved at various levels: it was not the same in Bernard and in Dante. Bernard often used the imagery of carnal love and even defended marriage, which he knew to be lawful and great, against those who attacked it, yet he never supposes it to be the final goal and plenitude of love. In St. Bernard as in other mystical poets—St. Hildegard, St. John of the Cross, for example—integration occurs at a very high level. It is a magnificent and daring endeavour to override the normal urge to satisfy emotional desire and to substitute the rational feelings. It is courageous to face life and self, constantly enlarging one's circle of love for God and man, admitting more and more human loves until all are fused in one luminous sphere of divine love. Such an undertaking can only be fulfilled if God's active grace calls a man to reality transcending any human sphere. It suffices to respond to the call to break out of the human circle to receive necessary grace and strength for gradual sublimation of human needs which are put to the service of Christ.

IV. *Mary and the Eternal Feminine*

Bernard had no experience of the physical expression of love, but he was conscious of its movings and could therefore speak so understandingly of it. Whatever may have been his poetic literary expression of love, he was never greatly drawn to anything but love of God alone. In the light of what has been said above, it is also quite conceivable that Dante spoke of love so divinely and so humanly. Both Bernard and Dante were—though in very different ways—at once carnal and rational. They were men who were aware of their feelings. The experiences each man had may have been different, but the process by which they transcended, went beyond them, was identical. Each had his own way of controlling his emotions and the way he expressed them, using them with constructive energy. Of all the love poets it is probably Bernard who speaks most movingly and most deeply of love, with an unsurpassed ardour, and a beauty of expression equalled only be Dante. Such combination of fervour and beauty could have no other fountain-head than the hidden source of divine love burning within him. Is it any matter for astonishment that at the close of the *Divine Comedy*, Dante should be led by Beatrice to such a mellifluent master of love and contemplation? And what could be more normal than for Bernard to lead Dante to a woman, that great Lady Mary of whom the Bride in the Song of Songs was a symbol and a prophetic anticipation.

Whether it be Beatrice, the Bride, or Mary, it is always a woman whom men like Bernard and Dante see to be the symbol of all that is best in themselves and all mankind. The mysterious finale of Goethe's *Faust*, so obviously reminiscent of the *Divine Comedy*, is an instant unveiled to reveal the part played by another woman, Margarethe: she leads Faust to Mary, who, in turn, draws him into the sphere of the Divine. Each choir in Paradise has its special song: the last word falls from the lips of the Marian Doctor who sings Mary's splendour and begs her to convert and draw to herself all that is best in Everyman. The final hymn of this *Chorus mysticus*, this *mystic choir*, contrasts the impermanent, as the Buddhists would say, with the eternal:

> All that is transient
> Is but a parable.
> The Inaccessible
> Here becomes Actuality.
> Here the Ineffable finds achievement.
> The Eternal Feminine
> Draws us upward.[16]

[1] The fact that the Sermon on the Song 39 gives direct inspiration to several passages of the *Divine Comedy* has been established by A. Masseron, *Dante et St. Bernard*, Paris, 1953, pp. 177-80. On the other hand, in order to write the great final prayer of the *Paradiso*, which will be mentioned further, Dante read St. Bernard's Sermons on the Annunciation, as has been shown by J. P. Deroy, 'Un acrostico nella preghiera di San Bernardo', in *Miscelanea Dantesca*, Utrecht, 1965, pp. 103-13. Cf. *Recueil d'études*, I, p. 211, and III, p. 194.

[2] *Par.* XXXIII. 145.

[3] *Inf.* II. 73.

[4] *Par.* X. 52-60.

[5] *Par.* XXXI. 109-11.

[6] *Par.* XXXIII.

[7] *Par.* XXXII. 128-9.

[8] *Par.* XXXIII. 120-1.

[9] *Par.* XXXIII. 145.

[10] *Vita Nuova*, XIX. 4.

[11] *Rime*, XX. 5.

[12] *Rime*, XVIII. 6-7.

[13] *Rime*, XLVI. 4.

[14] *Rime*, XLIX. 1.

[15] The context, at the end of *Le Monde Cassé*, gives full meaning to this idea: 'Ah! c'est comme si tu m'étais rendue après ta mort . . .—Ce mot-là, je vais maintenant tâcher de le mériter', quoted and commented on by G. Fessard, *Théâtre et mystère*, Preface to G. Marcel, *La soif*, Paris, 1938, p. 35. The theme appears again in *La soif*, ibid., p. 281: 'Par la mort, nous nous ouvrirons à ce dont nous avons vécu sur la terre.'

[16] *Goethes Werke*, ed. H. Kurtz, IV, Hildburghausen, 1870, *Faust*, Zweiter Theil, p. 365. Goethe's hymn becomes even more meaningful when contrasted with the parody of it written by Nietzsche:

> Welt—unabtrennliche
> Lasst uns sein!
> Das Ewig-Männliche
> Ziet uns hinein.

(Let us be inseparably of this world. The Eternal-Masculine draws us downward.), Allen Schaffenden geweiht, Herbst 1884, ed. and trans. A. Baümler, *Nietzsche Werke*, vol. 5, Leipzig, 1930, p. 509.

Index